ENDORSEMENTS

This is a story worth hearing, full of life and encouragement for every believer. Do yourself a favor. Open this book and receive a revelation towards helping you on your path to transforming your local school.

John Dawson
President Emeritus, YWAM international

Kris is one of those workers for God that takes initiative, finds opportunities, and makes the most out of them. Then, she multiplies that which she has been fruitful in. She is one of those humble people but is outstanding as a leader, making no fuss about it, but doing what she sees she can do. She has made an impact at a high school here in Hawaii that has been transformed from a place of high hostility and violence to a place of peace and learning.

I encourage not only Kris for writing this book but for everyone that reads it to pray for application and to get involved with high schoolers. It was at that age that David stood before Goliath. That Joseph was taken as a slave to Egypt. It was at that age that Daniel and his three friends were taken hostage to a foreign nation and they all became nation changers. Read, asking the Holy Spirit to show you what you can do, to change and see the transformation of nation changers in high schools near you.

Loren Cunningham
Founder, Youth With A Mission

I met Kris almost 25 years ago while leading a Youth with a Mission ministry in Portland, Oregon. I could tell she was an energetic young woman who was deeply committed to following Jesus and doing whatever God asked her to do. She had a heart to see God's kingdom come powerfully to the city, and especially our youth. When God led her back to North Portland, it was easy to join Kris and her husband, Randy, in prayer walks at Roosevelt High School. Eventually, our church provided a prayer canopy over one of the local middle schools that feeds in to Roosevelt.

Kris has shown herself to be faithful and consistent in her walk with Christ and her desire to follow Him wherever He may lead her and her family. It is the substance of her character that inspires me to fully endorse Kris as a person and to endorse the contents of her book.

Pastor Kelly Cohoe,
Grace Christian Fellowship
Portland, Oregon

For those in the faith community, it is no surprise that prayer can change people, schools, and communities. The transformation of Roosevelt High is an example of the miracle that happens when people come together selflessly to create a better world, one person at a time, one school at a time.

It was a joy to be on this journey with Kris.

Deborah Peterson, former principal of Roosevelt High School

When I heard that people had been praying for our students and staff by name, I was stunned. I shared this with my fellow teachers at our staff meeting. There also was stunned silence. We did not know how to respond, knowing that people cared so much about our students and ourselves that they actually took the time to pray for us by name. I felt blessed, truly blessed.

Sharon Langworthy, former mathematics teacher, Roosevelt High

When introduced to the "canopy of prayer" in 2005, I was very excited. Kris enthusiastically shared what was happening at my alma mater, Roosevelt High School. After joining her and others for a prayer walk at Roosevelt, I eventually followed her steps to organize a prayer canopy for Parkrose High School, where my children attended.

The canopy of prayer was a powerful, united force that had a great impact. Parkrose made strong community strides. Policies were changed at the district level, the football program turned around, and many parents and PTA groups stepped up to improve things.

In addition, the sense of unity we experienced as praying vessels was beautiful and touching. Just typing this is refueling my intercessor's heart. Prayer makes such a difference, and corporate prayer puts His angels to work. When calling out each student by name in prayer and personal focus, I believe a special touch of the Lord comes forth.

Pray on, warriors!

Jennifer Markham, parent who started the prayer canopy at her local school

In January, 2011 I met Kris on the beach in Kona, Hawaii. She shared about her involvement in prayer at Roosevelt High School. I was inspired by her story and went back home and talked with my pastor about starting a canopy of prayer to cover our high school in Oregon. He challenged me to include the elementary and middle school too. My concern was finding enough people to pray for that many students. I decided to cover the middle and high schools the first year (2011-2012). I had more people who wanted to pray and not enough cards to give them!

The next year I added the elementary school. People asked me to include the Christian school and another smaller school as well. I did. I still had people asking for a prayer card when I didn't have any left to give. Our schools did not have the challenges that Roosevelt had, so the results were not as dramatic. What amazed me was that in our small community we had nine churches covering five schools, praying for every student, teacher, coach, and staff for a whole school year! The results were: a growth in unity among our churches, increase in school attendance, decrease in suspensions, decrease in the dropout rate, improvement in grades, and an increase in the graduation rate. These are only a few indicators that can be measured. Only God knows what took place in the hearts of the people who prayed and who were prayed for! I challenge you to take up the mantle to organize a canopy of prayer for your schools and see what God will do.

This is the confidence we have in approaching God: that if we ask anything according to his will, he hears us. And if we know that he hears us—whatever we ask—we know that we have what we asked of him. I John 5:14-15

Paula Perkins
Sisters, Oregon

The Roosevelt High Story

KRIS RICHARDS

DEDICATION

This book is for the two unnamed mamas with Moms in Touch (now Moms in Prayer), International who met every week to pray for their children's schools back in 2004. They knew there was a vacuum of prayer for schools in North Portland. They decided to pray all year for a mom in that community to get a heart for Roosevelt High School. I am that mom. This whole book is because of those moms who prayed.

Kris Richards

CONTENTS

FORWARD.. xv

INTRODUCTION xvii

1. WHAT AM I DOING, AND HOW DID I GET HERE? 1

2. WE KNEW THE SCHOOL WAS BAD WHEN… 7

3. KICK-OFF OF A PRAYER MOVEMENT 13

4. NOTING NEHEMIAH 21

5. CATCHING THE VISION—A TRIP TO HAWAII 27

6. ENCOURAGEMENT AND MULTIPLICATION 35

7. THE SCHOOL WAS STARTING TO CHANGE
   AND SO WAS I.. 45

8. JUST THE RIGHT FIT.. 49

9. CHURCHES COME ON BOARD 57

10. "SURE, I CAN DO THAT!" 61

11. THIS NEEDS TO SPREAD ALL OVER
    THE DISTRICT! 71

12. THE BIG PICTURE 79

13. LESSONS LEARNED ALONG THE WAY 85

14. STARTING YOUR OWN PRAYER CANOPY 91

APPENDICES 99

AFTERWORD 112

Kris Richards

FORWARD

I remember when I first heard that all the students at our school were being prayed for...by name, by the local group of intercessors committed to the schools. My thought at the time was, "that's really nice." BUT, the impact of that effort had not yet become apparent to me. What would become evident as the weeks went on was this: As the schools were going through significant change—through the concerted effort of a praying group of people— a belief arose that it was possible to see change for the good.

The area had been known for gang problems and transient families. The high school football team seemed to be struggling from a lack of committed, grade-qualified players. Low test scores and keeping students in school was a significant problem. Added to that, it had become a magnet area for immigration. The face of the community was in rapid change...the dynamics of which were continually shifting.

A series of things would ensue and the way for a changed environment made ready. It would become evident that change was happening. Committed school leadership was set in place. Negative trends reduced—including—crime, gang activity, and suicidal type behaviors.

Even my own outlook changed dramatically. I came to see that it was possible to believe for the impossible. APPROPRIATING the belief that crime would be reduced actually resulted in crime being suppressed. Not theoretical change, but real change. Days would go by without any new incidences...except for follow-up on those that had occurred somewhere else and were being reported on campus. Negative trends would rise up, but be pushed back as prayer warriors engaged.

During those years at the high school, I came to believe we could actually take authority over crime and problems...and in fact, after appropriating that belief in prayer, subsequently there were no new significant problems in that environment while "on duty."

Bob Tallman,

Campus Police for Portland Public Schools—Parkrose High School

INTRODUCTION

From where I stood in my yard in North Portland, things didn't seem bad. At first. The boys next door helped us roof our home the year after we moved in. We helped send them to youth camp at our church. They'd chat with me while I watered my garden. As I did the dishes, I'd look out to see one boy pulling his bike out of my rose bush, or the older one strutting by with his buddy, khaki pants sagging.

Then one day I heard yelling. That buddy's mom was accosted by her boyfriend three doors down while she tried to pull out of the driveway. I called the police as I heard the man repeatedly yelling and throwing his fists down on top of the car. The bad part was the cops came to my front yard and loudly asked, "Which house is it??" So then I had to point it out---with the neighbor kids watching. At that point, they black-listed me. I was the Nark. The bad guy. The Nosy Neighbor who should let well-enough alone. But I couldn't.

When the older boy dropped out of Roosevelt High School, I was saddened. When the police dumped his horribly mangled car onto his front yard—feet from our house—I was shocked. When the cars lined our street full of mourning teens on their way to the funeral of that same buddy who never returned from that car wreck, I was moved. The neighbors could tell I cared. They invited us to join them at the funeral. Though I'd held my tongue before with those boys, I didn't at the funeral. A mic was set up for comments. I stood up. I cracked a few jokes about knowing the brand of underwear the boys wore as they sidled by my kitchen window every day.

And then, I went there: I offered a hope of knowing Jesus, telling the teen parents and the gangster wanna-be's that there was something more than this. Four hundred eyes respectfully listened to the mama on the block.

Then it was their turn. They grabbed the mic and joked about how they would light up a joint that night and remember their friend. "Let's have a toke for Tony!"

I was too late.

At the reception, Tony's mom opened up to me. Her son had always known he'd be dead before his 19th birthday. Tony died at 18. One consolation I had was that one teacher—his art teacher—had shared the Lord with Tony a few months earlier. It struck me how just one Christian could be a light in such a hurting community.

I drove home from the funeral with my husband, sobered by what I saw and heard. I figured most of these kids were drop-outs or were attending the alternative high school in North Portland where Tony had gone. How did these kids end up in this mess? Was there anything I could do about it?

A half mile from our home, our friends were trying to *do something* about the youth situation. They enrolled their daughter, Mary, at Roosevelt High. Mary was an honor student and a wonderful babysitter for our boys. She quickly was placed on varsity sports teams—perhaps because so few tried out for those teams. The teachers liked Mary. The students---not so much. She stood out as a blond-haired, light-skinned girl with two professional parents at home. As a Christian, Mary was trying to be light at Roosevelt High. But it was hard when every day she heard students call her

"F'in B----."

One day as she walked down the crowded hallway, a big boy decided to get her attention. Only, he chose a strange way to show it: the 6' 3", 275 lb young man picked her up by the neck, causing pain and fear to well up in Mary. When he didn't let go, she felt herself losing her ability to breathe. Her friend kicked him in the groin, and he let go. When the assistant principal finally arrived, she chided the friend for taking physical action first instead of finding help. Incensed, Mary's parents marched into the principal's office, demanding justice. They were told the boy was in foster care and needed some slack—he didn't really know what he was doing.

Later, when a girl kept telling Mary she hated her and wanted to kill her, Mary's dad contacted the police. "Are you sure you want to file a report?" The officer cautioned. "Things might not go well for your daughter from some of the rougher girls at the school."

That was the straw that caused Mary's family to withdraw their daughter from Roosevelt. They enrolled her at Wilson High School in the West Hills. Writes Mary's mom, "Roosevelt was such a horrible experience for us. We just had to find a school that was safe for our daughter."

That was the year before our story started—when we began praying concertedly for Roosevelt High. It was that school year that prompted the notoriety the next fall of getting on the "Ten Most Violent Schools" list for the state.

From where I stood in my rose garden in North Portland, the local school was in a heap of trouble. Much to my surprise, God was preparing me to do something about it.

Kris Richards

CHAPTER 1

WHAT AM I DOING, AND HOW DID I GET HERE?

Come on, Molly, where *are* you?" I gestured into the air towards my babysitter, wherever she might be. It was 2006. Our friend was due at our North Portland home ten minutes earlier to watch our small boys so I could attend the local neighborhood association meeting. She had been detained, which made me late, so that I came flying into the neighborhood meeting like some half-cocked tornado, supposed to be under-control for my presentation. The meeting was held at a local Catholic university. I came running up, feeling like Maria in *The Sound of Music*, putting the brakes on just enough to stop in the doorway. But unlike the prim and proper reception Maria had with the nuns, these men of the cloth were anything but. Leaning forward with enthusiasm, they stood in the doorway, huge smiles clad across their faces, welcoming me warmly.

"Would you like some wine?" they asked.

"No thanks," I replied.

"Please, Kris. Come in. Do tell us how we can help Roosevelt High School," one of the board members said.

Thus began a high-energy meeting which led to more meetings and opportunities to speak on the school I had come to love. How did I get here? I was a former public school teacher who chose to live in the neighborhood with my husband, raising our two young sons. I had a heart for the poor and "left-over kids" of North Portland and somehow, had become an authority. What I thought was a neighborhood meeting turned into a presentation before the leadership board of the university. This became a springboard for resources for Roosevelt, and an open door for further advocating across the city.

I drove away from that meeting shaking my head asking, "What am I doing and how did I get here?" I would ask myself that question several more times in the four years we prayed and served at Roosevelt. After a while, I stopped asking it. I realized that when you align yourself with the needy and outcasts, it becomes a fast-track for God's agenda. You just have to hang on, graciously step into your new role, and see where it takes you.

The upshot of that meeting was connecting the dots between the university and the high school down the street for scholarships and dreaming about bussing in kids for "A Day in the Life of a College Student." College was a concept as foreign to many of the students as a trip to Russia. The treasurer of the university invited me to a North Portland Rotary meeting, which accessed more resources for the school. I was astounded at what God was opening before me. It was like a big relay race, where one person runs for a ways, and then hands the baton off to the next person.

Recently, I was reading in the Bible about someone who reminded me of myself. Saul was an unlikely leader, an insecure chap who was God's choice for the Israelites' request for a king. He wasn't the greatest king, and we know what happened in his transition-gone-bad with David; but he was the one appointed for the job at that time. In 1 Samuel 9, Saul is a young man out looking for his father's lost donkeys. The servant remembers that a seer is in the nearby town. He suggests they ask the prophet Samuel about the donkeys.

Unknown to Saul, the Lord had spoken to Samuel the day before and said, "About this time tomorrow, I will send you a man from the land of Benjamin. Anoint him leader over my people Israel; he will deliver my people from the hand of the Philistines." Saul meets Samuel, opens his mouth to ask about the donkeys, and Samuel shocks him: Standing at the door, leaning forward, offering him a glass of wine, he says, "Go up ahead of me to the high place, for today you are to eat with me, and in the morning I will let you go and will tell you all that is in your heart." Saul is no-doubt confused. Samuel tells him not to worry about the donkeys. Saul walks into the eating hall as instructed, and there is a place next to the host just for him. Not only is there a place for him at this crowded table, but a large leg of meat had been set aside for him for this very meal. The next morning, Samuel anoints Saul's head and kisses him.

When Saul left, he was a new person, with a new identity. He'd been anointed by the man of God, and his footing was sure.

I believe there are many people who are called and anointed to lead who are out looking for donkeys. They come stumbling into meetings and can't believe that the people have been waiting for them. A place has been made and food has been set aside for that very time. Not just the people in the meeting are waiting, but the forgotten people out in the community, who are waiting for that insecure leader to grab the baton and to start running.

This is the story of one unlikely leader, a stay-at-home mom in a forgotten corner of Portland, who was willing to take the baton. It is about a prayer movement, an anointing passed on, a high school transformed, and a community that noticed.

FOR FURTHER REFLECTING:

Is there something that has been stirring in your heart for your community? Do you feel at times that there is something more for you to do with your life? Have you had nudges to lead something, but haven't been sure what it is? Jot down any stirrings you have been sensing...

_____

_____

_____

_____

_____

_____

_____

_____

_____

_____

"The Lord answered me: 'Write the vision; make it plain on tablets, so he may run who reads it" (Hab. 2:2 ESV).

And this could be your community.

Kris Richards

CHAPTER 2

WE KNEW THE SCHOOL WAS BAD WHEN...

Not long after I had spoken at the university, I had a dream in which I was driving our car along a road with a long stone wall. The wall continued for quite a distance along the right side of our car. Then it stopped at a fancy gate. My car pulled in to the gate, which opened automatically. I wondered what that was about.

A few weeks later, this dream came to life. As mentioned earlier, I had been invited to speak at the North Portland Rotary club by the treasurer of the University of Portland. He gave me directions to their luncheon location for their monthly meeting. As my older car snaked its way along a tall hedge along the Columbia River, finally the hedge broke free. There was a fancy stone gate with a sign announcing the country club where Rotary met. Just like my dream, I didn't have to have the combination or anything. The gate just opened before my car, and I entered the manicured grounds, blown away that I was seeing my dream in full-life.

I found my way to the clubhouse, where (much like the meeting at the university) men and women greeted me. They listened with earnest to my sharing about my observations of Roosevelt's dire needs, and asked how they might help. "We have funds set aside for projects like this. Can you advise us how to expedite them?" I provided a few contacts for them as I left.

I drove away from that meeting astonished at what God had set up. I was continuing to ask myself, "What am I doing and how did I get here?" Like Saul as he wandered in to the feast set aside for him, I walked into a room of strangers, a luncheon at a country club where I was the guest speaker. It was as if God had set a role for me to play and I just had to show up and play it.

I was starting to see that when He wants to adjust the course we are on, He goes to great lengths to communicate that to us—even causing dreams to come to life!

We knew that the high school was bad when our neighbor was told at parent-teacher conference time to get out while she could. "Your son will not grow here. Transfer him to another school," two teachers kindly said. So Barbara Thomas' daughter did choose to transfer to the prestigious St. Mary's girls' school downtown. But the son? No, Shaphan stuck around. Felt he was supposed to be there. That fourteen-year-old boy knew beyond a doubt that God had called him to remain at Roosevelt. That kid taught me something. Many other people became my "teachers" during that time, but Shaphan stood out with wisdom beyond his years.

I knew Shaphan Thomas from church. I knew he was from a single-parent family, and lived on the next street down from us. I had helped his mom out with a need a few years earlier in their small rental home. One day, while out for a walk with my husband, we noticed Shaphan walking around as well. We asked what he was up to.

"I'm praying."

"You are? We pray a lot for this area. What are you praying about?"

"This neighborhood and my high school."

We discovered that Shaphan chose to attend Roosevelt. We learned that he prayed on a regular basis for God to do something in St. Johns, and at the school where he was a freshman.

My husband and I were astonished to see a kid—especially a public school kid from St. Johns--with such vision and resolve. When we found out that he was holding a Bible study at the local McDonald's once a week for peers from his school, we told him we wanted in on his prayer-walking. We joined him a few times, and we began to want more for his high school. I realize now that we became part of the answer to that young man's prayers. (Side note: Shaphan Thomas is currently a successful public school teacher of junior high students in Central Oregon.)

St. Johns is a working-class community in North Portland. It is somewhat isolated as it is out on a peninsula over six miles from downtown Portland. Situated along the Willamette River, this town of 27,000 had one high school, two middle schools, and five elementary schools when this story was taking place (2005). There are historical registry churches, a library, a police station, and an old theater. The centerpiece is the St. Johns Bridge, similar in architecture to the Golden Gate Bridge. Here are facts from the 2000 census about St. Johns:

- Median age, 30
- 19% of residents were at the poverty level
- About 16% of men and women had a B.A. or higher
- Almost twice that amount had just a high school diploma.
- Ethnicity: 2/3 of the people of St. Johns were white, 14% were Hispanic, 9% were black, 6% were Asian.
- Median household income: $35,000
- Roosevelt High in 2005 was made up of three magnet schools: one for health occupations, one for arts communication and technology, and one for Spanish immersion.

The next school year after we talked with Shaphan was 2004-05. Good friends of ours thought they'd put their daughter into the school to see if they could bring light to this place where people were quickly jumping ship in the wake of the "No Child Left Behind" Education legislation. As George W. Bush had written it, any family in a school with poorer-performing test scores could transfer without hindrance to another school in their district with better test scores. It sounds great for the people who want a fighting chance for their kid. Roosevelt was regularly on the "Poor Performing" list, so anyone with initiative, or an automobile, or the pass for the city bus, transferred out. This meant that a school of 1500 went to 600 in a couple years.

No Child Left Behind was a bipartisan act of Congress started in 2002. States held each school accountable to make "Adequate Yearly Progress" on annual tests, and would not be deemed successful in passing those tests unless every people group of that school passed "the benchmarks." These standards were set by each state. Students in low-performing areas could have permission to move to higher-test results areas, or request tutoring if they were not passing at their school.   (From   Great!Kids   Education   Trends. www.greatschools.org/gk/articles/no-child-left-behind.) Roosevelt did have tutoring being offered through this program, as they were branded a "failing school."

The situation with our friend's daughter, Mary led to her leaving the school that spring. Many other students did as well.

So that next fall, the district decided that the principal had had his share of fence-sitting, and asked him to not come back. In his place, they hired a temporary principal, Mrs. Deborah Peterson. They didn't know it when they brought her on, but she was the best thing to ever happen to Roosevelt High.

We started up a prayer covering over the school that fall. Deborah Peterson came to see me as an unexpected ally. At first when things started turning around, I told her it was due to prayer.

She countered with, "We've worked hard."

I kept saying, "It was prayer."

She'd say, "We worked hard."

Years later, we would both acknowledge that the good started and kept happening ever since the army of 60 folks joined me praying for those 600 kids—and ever since she worked extremely hard as the head principal who would serve at the school for five years. But I'm getting ahead of myself.

WE KNEW THINGS WERE BAD the week we started the prayer canopy, the same week that Channel 12 News came out with "The Ten Top Schools to Watch for Violence in Oregon." Two of the schools were under the roof of Roosevelt High.

FOR FURTHER REFLECTING:

Have you ever noticed that the news can paint a bleak picture of a school or establishment? We can do the same thing with our words. Think about a person or a time when people spoke ill of a place, but you knew in your heart it was not that way.

_____
_____
_____
_____
_____
_____
_____
_____
_____

"The Spirit of the Sovereign Lord is on me, because the Lord has anointed me to proclaim good news to the poor. He has sent me to bind up the brokenhearted, to proclaim freedom for the captives and release from darkness for the prisoners, to proclaim the year of the Lord's favor …. and provide for those who grieve in Zion—to bestow on them a crown of beauty instead of ashes, and a garment of praise instead of a spirit of despair. They will be called oaks of righteousness, a planting of the Lord for the display of his splendor" (Is. 61:1-3).

CHAPTER 3

KICK-OFF OF A PRAYER MOVEMENT

L ady, if this school turns around, I'm joining your prayer movement!" I raised my eyebrows at the police officer standing next to me in the hallway. He went on to tell me what had transpired in the first six weeks of the 2005-2006 school year. It was shocking. I told him I would not repeat the information to the press. Let's just say that it was violent stuff. It involved a weapon, fights, and high-level drugs. "And that's an improvement from last year," he threw in.

How could *this* be better? How could people teach—or learn—in that kind of environment? In my nine years of public school teaching, I had never seen anything close to this. I began to see my local high school with new eyes.

I visited the Roosevelt High campus around mid-October, hoping to meet the principal. I wanted to introduce myself, tell her about our intentions, and to assure her that it would only be to pray for things to go well at her school. It was not to gain numbers for churches, or for Christians to proselytize. We wanted to find out what was *really* going on so we could pray for what the administration wanted to see changed.

13

The principal was unavailable, so I found the police officer, stationed on campus as part of the North Portland precinct. I figured things were pretty serious if the local precinct was housed inside the school. I told him that I needed baseline data to see where the school is now, and that I would return in a month to see if things had changed.

They had. Six weeks later, the officer told me, "There's been a 100% improvement in the leadership of this school since last year." But he said it takes a while for things to trickle down from the leaders to the students' behavior. "Don't take us off your prayer list," he added.

One assistant principal for the school attempted to tell me what was going on as the school year began. "Things are improving here. It is much better than last year. Please don't go back to your prayer people and tell them how horrible this school is; the paper gives us enough bad press as it is!" I assured her I would not, and that I'd tell them things were on the up-swing. When she saw I really cared, she agreed to request print-outs for me of the first names of the freshman class. Using public-access from last spring's yearbook, we had copied the first names down of the students and staff in order to pray for them. The incoming freshmen were not in those pages. I wanted to believe the positive message of this optimistic administrator.

Then I had the dream. It was the night that we kicked off the prayer canopy. It was the night that we took the names from that yearbook plus the new freshmen, lumped into groups of ten on little cards, and handed them out in piles to local pastors and parents, urging them to give them to people they knew would faithfully pray. We asked folks to pray privately once a week for things to change.

Praying with folks from the neighborhood and local churches.

In the dream, I was standing with a small group of people watching a twin-engine airplane. The plane was slowly circling around. As I watched more closely, I realized the plane was losing altitude and would soon crash. It got closer to me. I could see the name emblazoned across the side of the plane: "ROOSEVELT." A chill ran up my spine. I knew that this school was crashing and burning. We were watching it happen, doing nothing. It was worse than that principal was letting on. Much worse.

I woke up and knew what I needed to do. I didn't go to the press, nor did I get on the Roosevelt-bashing bandwagon. Instead, I got on the phone. I called up that handful of local pastors before their Sunday services started. I normally am not this bold of a person, but that dream grabbed my attention. We had to do something! "We gotta do more. I had this dream last night." I could hear my voice rising as I recognized that desperate times called for desperate measures. "We need to meet on that campus and walk around and pray. It's way worse than anyone's letting on." They all agreed, and immediately announced it to their congregations. We would meet the next Sunday to do a prayer walk.

I was pleased. A few months earlier when Randy and I had met with the St. Johns area pastors at a ministerial meeting to explain this prayer canopy, they had all shown interest. Several pastors let us know that—although they had vision for their churches—they lacked vision for doing anything in our local community. This was just the thing, they told me, to light a fire under their congregation in the way of caring for the local high school.

"Prayer Walking" was something popularized by prayer leaders such as England's Graham Kendrick and Youth With a Mission's John Dawson (*Taking our Cities for God*). Randy and I had read books by both of these men in the 90's and had participated in prayer walks for years. Some prayer walks were with intercessors from all over our city at an annual "March for Jesus" in Portland. We had led prayer walks with our church leadership when our church transferred from the commercial area of town into more of "The 'Hood" of NE Portland. We had found that when people walk the land and pray, they develop a heart for the area, they observe what is going on, and from those observations they can pray for blessing or pray in the opposite of negative things going on. For instance, if they notice that a street often has fighting or marriage arguments in the homes, they can pray in peace and blessings on households. Often, people who do prayer walks get insights into the spiritual climate that forms the backdrop for patterns of happenings in that area. They often develop such compassion from prayer walking that they end up volunteering to serve in that area.

On October 29th, 2005, a week after we kicked off the Roosevelt High School Canopy of Prayer at the local community center, we met on the campus. We were about 12 to 15 people from the neighborhood, including a few pastors, some parents, a Roosevelt grad, a woman from the neighborhood association, and my family. I now know that our little band made some significant headway that day. It happened as we walked in unity. It happened as we humbled ourselves before our God, crying out for Roosevelt. It happened as we prayed the Word of God back to our heavenly Father about this school that He had not forgotten.

"If my people, who are called by my name, will humble themselves and pray and seek my face and turn from their wicked ways, then will I hear from heaven and will forgive their sin and will heal their land." II Chronicles 7:14

Our boys with their "swords of the Spirit" pray for a break-through.

We prayed Joshua 1:3, where God tells young Joshua, "I will give you every place that you set your foot, as I promised Moses." (NIV) We also read aloud sections of Nehemiah. That's the story about the servant of the king who is distraught because the walls of Jerusalem had been torn down. He is so upset, that the king releases him to go lead a whole delegation to re-build the wall.

We particularly felt led to pray out Nehemiah 3. This is the part about the gates of the city being burned down. The gates of the city represent places of authority. We felt the Lord showing us that the authority of this high school had been broken down and needed to be built back up. We went to bat, asking God to re-build the authority of this school.

The next week, I asked the same administrator if she'd seen any changes at her school that week. "I've had a massive break-through with my staff," she said, not knowing why I was asking. I wasn't sure what she meant by a "massive break-through," but I was encouraged that our prayers for the leadership of the school were being answered. We also heard that week that the Portland School Board had made Deborah Peterson the new permanent head principal of Roosevelt High. As I said earlier, she was the best thing to ever happen to that school.

We began to think that this was working! Like the passage we had prayed in Nehemiah, the "gates of the city" were being re-built! There was nowhere to go but up, right? I decided I'd seen enough to keep going, and resolved to pass on any information of progress (or problems) via email to the pastors and leaders who had taken those prayer cards. I wanted to keep this band of intercessors informed and motivated to *keep* praying!!

We had the privilege of being back-seat riders to what God was up to in our midst. It was a ride that was soon to become faster and wilder. I'd learn to hang on with all my might.

FOR FURTHER REFLECTING:

Have you ever done a prayer walk? It's a simple idea. Joshua was told that God would give him wherever he placed his feet. Talk with friends about going somewhere in your community to pray. It is not for show, but could just look like people going on a walk around the edges of a piece of land, talking softly. In reality, you are blessing that area. You are contending for what needs changing as God reveals it to you, praying instead for a blessing in that place. Write down what issues or patterns need turning around in that place.

_____

_____

_____

_____

_____

_____

_____

_____

"I will give you the keys of the kingdom of heaven; whatever you bind on earth will be bound in heaven, and whatever you loose on earth will be loosed in heaven" (Matt. 16:19).

CHAPTER 4

NOTING NEHEMIAH

O n that first and significant prayer walk we had around the high school, we read from Nehemiah and prayed similar prayers of rebuilding the wall and the "gates of the city" that had been burned. Now as I read through Nehemiah 1, I draw more meaning for those of us who care about our local school.

It begins in verse three. His brothers return from visiting the Jewish remnant, the exile in Judah. Nehemiah asks how they are doing. He **hears** that "those who have survived are in *great trouble* and *disgrace*" (emphasis is mine). The wall is broken down and the gates are burned. What does Nehemiah do? 1) He weeps. He is sad to hear this news about the condition of a place and a people that he is close to. He allows himself to get a burden from the Lord for this situation. 2) He prays. He reminds God that He is a God who keeps his covenant of love with those who love him and obey his commands. He asks that God's ear be attentive and his eyes be open to hear the prayer of his servant. He reminds God of his promise to them, that if they are unfaithful, He would scatter them among the nations. But if they return to Him and obey him, even if the people are in

21

exile, He would gather them and bring them to the place God has chosen for them (v. 8-9). So then he asks God to be attentive to him and the other servants who still delight in revering God's name. 3) He asks for success in terms of favor in the presence of this man (v. 11). "This man" is the king, King Artaxerxes, for whom Nehemiah works as the cup-bearer.

In Chapter two, his boss the king notices that his face is sad. He allows the king to hear of his heart for his people. "Why should my face not look sad when the city where my fathers are buried lies in ruins, and its gates have been destroyed by fire?" (2:2) So he identifies with the city of his fathers. That is like the school of your own neighborhood. We actually identified with the things going on at that school and asked God to forgive people for those things, such as neglect, or lack of strong leadership, etc. Nehemiah allowed himself to be sad about this, and to share his burden with the person who was in authority. The king asks him what he wants, and Nehemiah asks nicely if he can go and visit that city of his fathers and rebuild the wall. He not only asks for this, but asks for the king to get letters from the nearby kings in order to have permission to get access to the land.

I feel there is a principle we can glean. Though he was frightened, he went to the top. He addressed the leaders of that land and asked permission. With each person who has started a prayer canopy, we have let the principal or someone in authority know that we are praying. We have asked them of what needs they perceive to still exist. Then, we get access to the yearbook and "the land" to go and survey it, to pray over it, and maybe see open doors to serve as the school administration sees that we truly care. We don't skirt asking the authority, we go right to them.

Next, he gathers a little group and visits the land.

Nehemiah goes to the land and surveys it. He really *sees* what is broken, what is so destroyed that his horse can't even cross, and what needs rebuilding. He recognizes what God put on his heart (v. 12) to do. Then, he invites those people to join him in rebuilding. He says in v. 17, "You see the trouble we are in: Jerusalem lies in ruins, and its gates have been burned with fire. Come, let us rebuild the wall of Jerusalem, and we will no longer be in disgrace."

This reminds me of when Jesus *saw* the crowd and *had compassion (Matthew 14:4).* The Greek word for saw **horáō,** means to *stare at, to discern clearly* (physically or mentally), to *attend to, to experience* (Blue Letter Bible). He truly looked at the people who were hungry. Or who were lame. Or who were lost. His seeing was knit with compassion— and always resulted in action. He stretched out his hand and healed, or he asked for a lunch to bless and multiply, or he touched them or taught them (Matthew 9:36, 14:14, 20:34, Mark 6:34). Are you willing to truly see those people or that hurting school in your community? Watch out! It might lead to you being compelled by love to act or to experience—not just to pray!

So, in summary, Nehemiah:

- **hears** of a need
- allows himself to **be burdened or sad** about the need
- **prays** about it
- **gets something that God puts on his heart** of what he is supposed to do
- goes and **sees for himself** the need
- **tells others** of the need
- **invites them to join him** in it----to bring the people out of trouble and disgrace.

That is what we are doing. No more disgrace of a bad reputation school. No more trouble of sunken test scores and high crime and low parent participation. Newspaper articles about Roosevelt went from all negative, to all positive. Test scores growth went from extremely low to the highest in the city. From zero Advanced Placement classes to many. It was a team effort, from people who heard, who saw, who felt, who prayed, and a God who answered.

FOR FURTHER REFLECTING:

The story of Nehemiah has to do with a regular guy who feels sad about something not right in his community. The "something" was that the wall had been broken down and was rubble. Instead of being strong and a protection around the city, it was a dilapidated laughing stock. He was so troubled about it that his boss released him from work to go do something about it. Is there a burden on your heart, a type of wall or gate that needs re-building? I've noticed that when it's God, the burden doesn't go away. It gets stronger. Pay attention! What is it you are deeply troubled about that is broken? Can you do something to rebuild or rally the troops? Pray and see what God shows you. It might include action!

_____

_____

_____

_____

_____

_____

_____

_____

"I was very much afraid, but I said to my king, 'May the king live forever! Why should my face not look sad when the city where my fathers are buried lies in ruins, and its gates have been destroyed by fire?'" (Neh. 2:2b-3)

"Then I said to them, 'You see the trouble we are in: Jerusalem lies in ruins, and its gates have been burned with fire. Come, let us rebuild the wall of Jerusalem, and we will no longer be in disgrace'" (Neh. 2:17).

Kris Richards

CHAPTER 5

CATCHING THE VISION—A TRIP TO HAWAII

You may be wondering how this prayer canopy started. It was through God getting our attention in supernatural ways. I was beginning to form a theory about the Lord. When He wants us to change the course we are on, He goes out of his way to communicate with us that something new is coming. We see this in the Bible with leaders like Moses when God spoke through the burning bush, or Abraham when God sent two messengers to speak about the son he would have. I started to experience first-hand how He uses supernatural means to speak into our lives, just like in the Bible times of old.

It was July of 2005. We had gone to Hawaii for our tenth anniversary. We were staying in the studio apartment of a lovely home near Kona and decided to visit the Youth With a Mission (YWAM) campus or "base" in town. We'd been there once before on a brief vacation. We knew we were called to the mission field eventually, and thought we might investigate the campus. We were excited to do this, as it's one of the main hubs for YWAM around the world.

Prior to our going to Hawaii, I had seen a picture or a

vision several times in prayer. It was a large white canopy over something. I couldn't tell its purpose, but it reminded me of the large *Cirque de Soleil* tents that I'd seen popping up in Portland and surrounding cities. In the vision, Randy and I were always holding up the top part of the canopy, and leaders we knew from around town were holding down the corners. I felt it was a covering or some kind of leadership for something, but I did not know what. I saw this picture a handful of times in that year, usually when I'd be in prayer.

A few days prior to our leaving for Hawaii, I'd written in my journal the following entry: "I know that we are called to the nations Lord, but I think Hawaii has something to do with it."

With Loren Cunningham, founder of YWAM

Imagine my astonishment, then, when we visited the YWAM base and found that the public gathering was that night, and that the founder of YWAM, Loren Cunningham was speaking. How much more was I intrigued when he seemed to read from my journal later in the evening: "You may think you're here by accident, but there's a call to the nations on your life, and Hawaii has something to do with it!" God had my attention! I silently threw my hands up in the air, greatly moved.

God got Randy's attention. As our plane landed on Oahu en route to the Big Island, Randy had quoted aloud from Isaiah 49:1 "Listen to me, you islands; hear this, you distant nations: Before I was born the Lord called me; from my birth he has made mention of your name."

So in the same meeting where Loren read my mail, so to speak, he also quoted from Randy. His only text for the evening's teaching was---Isaiah 49:1. Now God had Randy's attention. Both of us sat there, riveted, tears running down our faces. We asked our old friend Rita Redeau, with whom we'd worked at a youth drop-in center in Portland, if we might have a chance to speak with Loren. "You can try," she said. "But he's awfully busy."

It looked highly unlikely. It was Loren's 70th birthday that night, and there were plans in place for the crowd of around 500 to eat cupcakes afterwards. Loren had just had knee surgery, so was gathering his crutches to get off the stage. We stood back-stage, waving to two young men who were assisting him. "Can we talk with him?" we tentatively asked.

The young men hesitated. But Loren saw us, and nodded his head. He hobbled down the ramp, and we quickly asked if we might chat with him. "Would you like to sit somewhere comfortable?" we asked.

He nodded his head. "Yes, I'll sit in my van. You see,

before I left my home this afternoon, the Lord gave me a picture. I was sitting in my van, praying for a couple with my hands out the window. I believe you are that couple." And that's exactly what happened. Loren climbed into his van, his wife Darlene beside him, and he listened to our story.

"We're visiting from Portland for our tenth anniversary. We both feel called to missions, and have had some experience with YWAM. Is there a way we can find out more about this base?" He told us he could set up informational interviews for us. We asked about Transformation Hawaii, which we'd heard about en route. We had heard about some movement of prayer that was sweeping across the Hawaiian Islands.

"Transformation Hawaii is way bigger than YWAM. There's a couple on this base who have relatives who started this up. We can introduce you to them." We asked him to pray for us, that God would lead us. With that, this 70-year-old world-renowned leader of the mission that we would one day join, stretched his arms out his window, laid hands on us, and prayed for God to mightily lead us.

This scene played repeatedly in our minds as we recounted this story to astonished friends over the months that followed.

Loren introduced us to his administrative assistant, who helped set up interviews with various leaders on the base. But when we met with Paul Chinen, whose brother and nephew started up Transformation Hawaii, our course shifted.

That independent young Daniel from Castle High is now married and pastors at the local church with his own family on Oahu.

Paul and his wife, Doreen, sat in a gazebo on the YWAM campus, overlooking the bay in Kailua Kona. Paul, who had grown up on Oahu, was a football coach at a local high school on the Big Island. With his spiked hair and cool shades and tattoos, we could tell he was a bridge-builder to the local youth. They told us how one teenager, their nephew Daniel, had noticed that his high school was escalating in violence and had wanted to see that change. Daniel had heard about Ed Silvoso, an evangelist from Argentina. After dividing up his city in Argentina and having people walk and pray those sections, Ed had seen revival hit, and statistics actually change for his city. Daniel wanted to see this for himself.

Daniel decided to go to Argentina in the summer before his senior year. But his baseball coach threatened to bench him in his last year if he did so. Daniel went anyway. He returned inspired by what he had seen—and wanted to try it out at his school. Daniel brought transformation to Castle High School. With his pastor father and friends, they conducted prayer walks and divided up the student body onto prayer cards which they handed out to folks to pray. He would later tell me that sitting on the bench his senior year was nothing compared to what God did in his community.

Paul and Doreen Chinen showed us a short DVD showing the results of that prayer at Castle High: all behavior problems were cut in half at the school. Fights among girls were eliminated. After a prayer walk one evening focusing on the drug problem, two major drug busts happened at the high school by noon the next day! So many people wanted to pray in that community on Oahu, that soon they were praying for the janitors and the secretaries, then the local fire department and the police officers. Prayer walks happened around their city, and crime statistics decreased.

Randy and I were astounded. Could this happen in Portland? At the same time, we both sensed from the Lord that we were to try this out with Roosevelt High School in Portland. "This is a transferable anointing," Doreen told us. I wasn't exactly sure what that meant, but it sounded like something I wanted. "Can we pray for you to take it to Portland?" This humble couple laid hands on us, and something was lit in our hearts. As we got ready to go, Doreen said, "This is a huge canopy of prayer over the islands."

"Did you say, 'canopy?'" I asked in surprise. It was indeed--the very thing I kept seeing in prayer! In fact, the change was so huge on Oahu, the County of Honolulu posted a letter online, stating that the "Canopy of Prayer" shall be allowed in every school in the state. Time would be allotted after school on every island in Hawaii for people to come in, walk, and pray. A video would later be made of Deputy Lieutenant Governor Duke Iona leading his state in this prayer, which was simulcast across Hawaii, uniting God's people for their local schools.

What did we have to lose? We would try it out at our local high school. And we had our name: the Portland Schools Canopy of Prayer. We thought we were visiting the YWAM base to find out about mission work, but God had other more immediate plans for us. In retrospect, we could see that He had given us a mission field—right in our own backyard.

FOR FURTHER REFLECTING:

Teen-ager Daniel Chinen gave up his senior year of baseball in order to pursue a higher calling, visit Argentina and take a radical prayer model back to his high school. Reflect on a time it seemed that you were missing out on something, but you traded that experience in for something better God had for you. Did it get bigger than your first little track you were on? Did you see later how God was leading you?

_____
_____
_____
_____
_____
_____
_____
_____
_____
_____

Read or peruse Gen. 37-47, the story of Joseph. Though he was sold into slavery, God had something better. Don't think small with the problems in your life! Consider how God might exchange those hardships for something far-reaching and long-term in its effect.

CHAPTER 6

ENCOURAGEMENT AND
MULTIPLICATION

Not long after I arrived back in Portland, I called Cal Chinen, the brother of Paul and the pastor who started that first prayer canopy on Oahu with his son. I'll never forget that call. I was parked on the side of the street by the YMCA in St. Johns, the community where we lived. Later I learned that homeless kids—who made up 37% of the population of Roosevelt High—lived at that YMCA.

Taking on this at-risk school brought butterflies to my stomach. Cal spoke reassuringly to me. Like Samuel the prophet to Saul, he encouraged me that we absolutely were able to lead this. Cal told me to stay close to the school leaders and he'd stay in touch with me. That conversation started a friendship between Cal, his wife Joy, and my husband and me that continues to this day. I called Cal about every few months in that first year to check in. An always-encouraging coach, he would cheer me on. "This is amazing, Kris! *Keep going!*"

A year later, we were ready to multiply this prayer

canopy. A Presbyterian pastor started praying for the local elementary school, and two urban pastors were praying for two middle schools—all of which fed to Roosevelt. Some local moms were willing to kick it off at Parkrose High and Parkrose Middle School where their children attended. Another pastor from a Church of God in Christ behind the high school offered to continue prayer for Roosevelt after our family moved to Vancouver.

When I told Cal about this growth, he was surprised and wanted to meet these leaders. Soon he'd be visiting the Portland area, and wondered if we could bring them all together for him to address them. Again, the memory of that time is ingrained in my head. Our missions pastor and friend helped me be a bit creative. I asked him to find me a copy of the theme song from "Rocky." We bought relay race batons from a sports store and wrote the name of each church and its local school with permanent ink on each baton. I think we had six or eight that I was to hand-off that day. The prayer canopy--a movement in Hawaii--was becoming a movement in Oregon.

An avid runner, I jogged in with my running gear and handed off each baton to the pastors and leaders, the Rocky music blaring. I know it sounds cheesy, but they were inspired. Cal addressed them passionately, and I remember my urban pastor friends Omari Jones and Kelly Cohoe leaning forward to hear all he had to say. They heard how God started it on Oahu, and how it had spread to the other islands. Cal told them how different spheres of the city of Kaneohe were now being prayed for, like the fire department and police force. They were seeing change. Cal was blown away by the results we had seen at Roosevelt after one year. He told us to *keep going*. The leaders came away super-charged. Cal had blown upon the fires that God had already ignited. And the movement spread.

At "Light up the Night" at West Albany High

A few months later, my friend Kathy in Albany was ready to start a prayer canopy down the Willamette Valley. I drove the hour and a half to meet with her group. About fifty young people were present, hailing from Young Life and a few churches in that small town. It was a warm September evening by the football field of West Albany High School. Instead of a track baton, I carried a lit candle, which I transferred to Kathy. She then turned to the teens and parents and lit their candles. Tiny points of light spread in the darkness. We worshipped, invited God's presence, and then walked in small groups all around the campus, praying for every inch of it. I drove back up I-5 confident that God would do great things in Albany as he'd already done in Portland.

About two years after we started praying for Roosevelt High School, someone intriguing came to town. George Otis Jr. is an author and speaker from the Seattle area who is famous for his Transformation video series. My husband and I had seen most of the videos, filmed in several nations, documenting stories of whole communities changed by prayer and unity in the body of Christ. I had heard he was coming and that he wanted to meet with leaders in the area to share stories of transformation in Portland. How could I get to that meeting? Unfortunately, by the time I heard of it, the deadline had come and gone for people to sign up to share. A pastor friend at the Foursquare church invited me to the roundtable meeting with the ~500 pastors and leaders from the region. I figured I would come and just listen and hear stories about the Northwest. But God had other plans.

West Albany High School

I actually don't remember much about that meeting other than we were sitting at large round tables with about eight people per table. We were in the former hotel that a creative church had taken over and made into a meeting hall—with a hotel business on the side. We had just had a snack break and I was taking a bite of some chocolate when the emcee asked, "Does anyone else have anything they'd like to share?"

Here was my chance! I couldn't let it pass by. I shot my hand up. I was called on, chocolate and all. Awkwardly, I finished the bite in my mouth before speaking, cracking an inadvertent joke in the process. Pastors laughed and waited to see what this persistent woman had to say. "I'd like to share what happened at Roosevelt High here in North Portland." People listened with polite attention. As I kept speaking, they leaned forward in their chairs. When I finished, they applauded what God did at Roosevelt High. At the next break, they bombarded me. Pastors from Olympia, Washington, the coast, down to Salem, Oregon inquired if they could start it up at their local high school.

"Of course you can, just do what we did!" I replied.

"Can you call me about it? Can I talk to you about this further?" Several pressed their business cards into my hand. I left the meeting astonished, again, at what God had done. It wasn't my savvy planning that got me the floor at that meeting. He made the way!

As I walked out of that roundtable meeting, one gentleman caught up with me in the parking lot. "Kris! Can I talk to you a minute? I run a Christian radio station in Portland. What you shared in there had such dramatic results, I wonder if this could be something we could adopt for the upcoming National Day of Prayer? I bet Shirley Dobson [of Focus on the Family, who heads up the national prayer day] would love to hear this story!" I was surprised and a bit embarrassed. *Was this guy for real?* He was so excited about what had transpired. I wasn't sure what to think of this.

I am embarrassed to admit now that I never followed up with that manager from the radio station. Maybe I was being Saul-like and timid. It was intimidating to think of being interviewed on the radio to start something happening at a national level. Later our paths would cross in prayer initiatives around the city, and I found that this gentleman was no longer managing the radio station. I missed that window of opportunity.

I confess that I wasn't able to personally follow up with those pastors and share more details of how this model works. Maybe I needed to be more organized with my time as by then I was teaching sixth grade and had two active sons. Perhaps I needed a secretary. This book is an answer to that quandary, of how to get the word out, to re-tell this story that begs to be told. I have seen that this is not about my noble efforts, it's about God. He is perfectly able to keep a good thing going without our marketing and human efforts!

Fast-forward several years to when we moved from the Portland area to Kona, Hawaii to serve with YWAM. One evening my husband and I were enjoying a sunset at a local beach, a small patch of sand and grass a few yards from the YWAM base. We ran into some friends from YWAM Salem. Dwayne and LeeAnne Rawlins introduced us to their friends, Paula and Dave Perkins, visiting from Sisters, Oregon. Dwayne told Paula about what we started up in North Portland. Paula is a prayer warrior for her area as well, frequently praying for Sisters High School where her husband teaches.

She wanted to hear our story. When I had shared the short version of it, she and her husband asked if I could come by their condo the next morning to tell more. They would be leaving soon for Oregon and wanted to hear the full account of what God had done and what part we had played. So we did. We met for coffee the next morning in their beautiful condo. I told all, and they took all… to Central Oregon!

The first year, they prayed for Sisters High School student-by-student. The next year, they prayed for every public and private school in their town. The superintendent informed Paula that there had been a 50% decrease in behavior issues in the year they'd been praying. Paula and her little band of praying moms continued to intentionally pray and walk around the schools of Sisters. Recently, she told me they now pray for the police and fire departments as well.

All we did was showed up at the beach to watch a sunset. God did the rest!

FOR FURTHER REFLECTING:

In the Genesis creation account, God created the different elements of the earth by speaking them out. He spoke them into existence and then he made provision for each creature to multiply. He told Adam and Eve to be fruitful and multiply. What does this mean for us? When you partner with God to bring about a new thing on this earth, you are co-creating with Him. Inherent in that new ministry should be an ability to keep going, to multiply. Who has God brought into your life who is sharing your burden? Could you find a way to speak about it, share the story of how your little corner of the earth started changing, and then pass that on to others? Whether it's with track batons, lit candles, or just bringing people together to pray over them and bless them, let it be carried on and continued! Brainstorm with the Lord what creative form this might take for you.

_____

_____

_____

_____

_____

"Taking the five loaves and the two fish and looking up to heaven, he gave thanks and broke the loaves. Then he gave them to his disciples to distribute to the people. He also divided the two fish among them all. They all ate and were satisfied, and the disciples picked up twelve basketfuls of broken pieces of bread and fish. The number of the men who had eaten was five thousand" (Mark 6:41-44).

CHAPTER 7

THE SCHOOL WAS STARTING TO CHANGE—AND SO WAS I

The year before we started this prayer canopy, I had gone to the (former) principal to see about a job. As a school teacher at home with small children, I had a couple afternoons a week I could come tutor. The principal's response? "I'd love to hire you, but I don't have any money." I thanked him, and turned on my heels. It didn't even dawn on me that I might volunteer there.

Now, less than a year later, I had such a love for this high school that I was starting to pray for any way to get onto that campus! I wanted to see the people I was praying for. I wanted to serve in any way I could. My heart had been changed. Money was no longer the issue.

Four days after I started to pray for a way to get onto the campus, my schedule changed. I had one afternoon free a week! I strolled on to the Roosevelt High school campus to see how I might help. I remember taking in every sight and sound of the school. The sun was cracking through the clouds on a warm March day. Crocuses were poking up in the beauty bark surrounding the three-storied, vintage-looking building.

Suddenly, I thought of a young man who had worked on the Roosevelt campus from our church. Craig Smith had tirelessly worked to help some of the poorest kids in that school. At that moment, I sensed the Lord whisper, "You are the next Craig Smith." I was floored. "Really, Lord?" He was a huge influence around here. A gutsy guy, Craig had spent several years working with kids in the inner-city. He wasn't afraid of the toughest kids or the roughest neighborhoods of Portland.

When I began working in the office filing papers, I wondered if *I* was in the roughest neighborhood. The secretary was nervously talking on a walkie-talkie radio. I kept filing, wondering what was going on. The secretary told me that a guy from the streets was running around on the third floor with a knife. "He has a scar from here to here," she indicated, dragging her index finger from one ear to the other.

Turns out he was a former student, looking for someone with whom he needed to settle a score. I scrunched down in my chair, and began praying as hard as I could under my breath. I was thinking, "Wow! This is my first day here. What do these secretaries have to put up with daily?" I began to wonder if I was in a war zone.

Something buzzed over the walkie-talkie from the police officer on campus. "Great! I'm glad you got him," the secretary called out in relief.

At the end of my first day volunteering on campus, I emailed the pastors who had taken the prayer cards, pleading for more prayer. This school was worse than I thought. We needed to be storming heaven for this place!

Roosevelt High School

FOR FURTHER REFLECTING:

I began to realize that my heart was changing as I prayed for this high school. I wasn't in it just for the money. In fact, I wasn't asking for any money! Yet I "struck gold" by seeing so many times God come through and answer what I was asking for on behalf of the students and staff at that needy high school. State a time when you noticed your heart become softer and less selfish about something or someone because you took the time to pray. God is faithful!

_____

_____

_____

_____

_____

_____

_____

_____

_____

_____

For it is God who is at work in you, both to will and to work for His good pleasure" (Phil. 2:13).

CHAPTER 8

JUST THE RIGHT FIT

A principle we learned from this prayer covering was that what I was offering needed to match the needs of the school. When I wasn't sure what to give, I would pray and see what God brought to mind. I'd try to use whatever gift He gave me to pull out and use for that particular situation. Why waste my limited time or my resources? I only wanted to do what God was leading me to do. Of course, this is how Jesus operated, only doing what the Father told him. It's really how we have to be as busy moms, isn't it? Do we honestly have time or money to waste?

One day, I felt led to let the assistant principal, Claire (not her name) know that I was thinking of her and praying. From my backyard, I cut a bouquet of lavender, dark purple, and white lilacs and placed them in a simple vase. I stopped by the office with a calligraphy note that said, "Just letting you know I'm thinking of you. I have your back covered." She froze in the doorway of her office. Her eyes misted as she opened up to me. *"Thank you!* These are my favorite flowers! These are just the kind my grandmother used to grow!" I strode out of that school, smiling at how God had helped me make her day.

Sometimes prayer itself was the actual need. Early in the year, I arrived to file papers in the school office. The secretary, a member of an inner-city church, pulled me aside. She took me into a side room and shut the door. Then, she proceeded to confess to me a sin to which she was enslaved. I listened, hugged her, and prayed with her for forgiveness. I returned to my filing, shocked at what had just happened.

Was this because of me? I don't think so. Yes, I was present, but I was the person on the ground while 60 people were praying in the background over their kitchen sinks or coffee tables. Because of *their* prayers—and God choosing to answer those prayers--I was seeing fruit before my eyes. I was simply the tip of the spear of their fervent intercession. God is so good!

One day I was folding laundry in my home. I quietly prayed for the high school and for that same assistant principal. In my mind's eye, I saw a picture of her high up on a shelf. Below the shelf, hands were reaching up and grabbing to pull her down. I didn't know what to do with this picture. I decided to put out a fleece. I said, "God, if you want me to share this with her, then cause me to run into her alone in that school the next time I go there."

I drove in the next Monday, did my filing work, and started to head out. School was out, and the halls were empty. The Lord reminded me of the vision I'd had. Suddenly, a side door opened. Out came Claire, the assistant principal. That was my cue. "Hi Claire," I said. "Can I share with you something?" She nodded, obviously in a hurry. "Sometimes when I pray I get an impression about people…" She stopped and nodded slightly, as if she could buy that. I began to share with her the picture I had, trying not to

50

stumble over my words. She stopped walking and her eyebrows raised. As I kept sharing, she leaned against the wall, giving me her undivided attention.

She nodded in recognition at what I shared. "Let's just say that my job here is not that secure!" Claire thanked me for sharing, then hustled out the door.

"But thanks be to God, who always leads us in triumphal procession in Christ and through us spreads everywhere the fragrance of the knowledge of him." II Cor. 2:14

This makes me think of further down in I Samuel 9, after Saul meets the prophet Samuel. Samuel tells him specific details of what will happen next as he walks home. This includes how the donkeys will be found, and how he will come upon a company of prophets. "The Spirit of the Lord will come upon you in power, and you will prophesy with them; and you will be changed into a different person. Once these signs are fulfilled, do whatever your hand finds to do, for God is *with* you (I Samuel 10:6,7). "

I'm not a prophet. But I believe that in that season—in that leg of the relay that I was running—God anointed me for that position. He gave me the ability to see things when I was at the high school serving, to observe and to discern things going on in the spirit. It was so that I could better pray and inform others to pray. I believe he gave me that prophetic picture for that assistant principal in order to encourage her.

Without getting off on a whole tangent about spiritual gifts, we have to be motivated by love with whatever gifts God gives us. I've been chewing on I Cor. 13 lately. That whole list of attributes about love follows the section on the illegitimacy of prophecies and eloquent tongues if we lack love. But it's framed out by the first verse in chapter 14: "Follow the way of love and eagerly desire spiritual gifts, especially the gift of prophecy." I'm just saying that if you are seeking after the God of love, and you love because He first loved us, then you will walk in love. And that might at times mean having a word or a picture for people whom we are called to love, or the people for whom you've been praying. What are you going to do if that happens? Will you act on it if He leads you?

During that season serving at Roosevelt High, God was instructing me in lessons about the supernatural. Like Saul, I prophesied, but eventually I saw that God blessed "whatever my hand found to do" with that high school. To Him be the glory! Here's another example of His blessing what my hand found to do.

A few weeks later, I noticed the school counselor walking by in the office. Her eyebrows were furrowed, her eyes were sad, and her lips were taut. I didn't want to guess the deep level of problems she was carrying at that school. After she walked out of the office, I mentioned to the secretary (the same one I'd prayed for earlier) how oppressed the counselor seemed. She agreed.

"Shall we pray for her?" I offered.

"Oh yes! Let's go in her office!" The secretary knew something about fervent prayer. Together, we bound depression and anxiety and heaviness and prayed in the opposite: peace, joy, and wisdom for this struggling counselor.

The next week when I came in to volunteer, that secretary was bursting with excitement. "I've been waiting every day until Monday when I'd see you again! That woman is a changed person! After we prayed, her face literally changed. It became soft again and she seemed at peace. I went into her office and told her a woman from the community who volunteers here had prayed for her, for a lifting of all that heaviness. She burst into tears."

I love how Peter talks about this gifts-working-towards-demonstrating-love.

The end of all things is near. Therefore, be clear minded and self-controlled so that you can pray. Above all, love each other deeply, because love covers over a multitude of sins. Offer hospitality to one another without grumbling. Each one should use whatever gift he has received to serve others, faithfully administering God's grace in its various forms. If anyone speaks, he should do it as one speaking the very words of God. If anyone serves, he should do it with the strength God provides, so that in all things God may be praised through Jesus Christ. To him be the glory and the power forever and ever. Amen.

I Peter 4:7-11

Sometimes what you go to offer becomes something much more as the needs of the school ebb and flow. By just showing up with your little gift in hand, you get to participate in something far greater. Such as what happened to my friend Cliff Chappell, who pastors the All Nations Church of God in Christ a block away from Roosevelt. A former successful businessman, Cliff had wanted to be a guest speaker for some of the students at the school. He had approached Claire about speaking, but she didn't seem interested in this middle-aged pastor coming to speak to her students. Cliff just kept praying for a door to open.

In the meantime, Pastor Cliff realized that many of his parishioners wanted to learn Spanish. He set up an arrangement with the school to allow a few Hispanic students to come teach at his church over several weeknights. The language classes met a need at his church and forged a trust with that assistant principal.

When he returned a few weeks later to thank this administrator for the excellent language work her students had done, she said, "Maybe I will let you speak to our students." What she didn't know, and Cliff couldn't know was that the timing of his visit would be perfect. The afternoon before Cliff came, two Hispanic siblings who had recently transferred away from Roosevelt were killed in a car crash. The students and staff were shell-shocked. Who was their speaker the next day? It was Pastor Cliff Chappell, who had seen his share of tragedies and youth dying before their time.

Cliff was able to listen to them, honor their grief, share stories of what he had seen in the community, and inspire the students to set goals and stay in school towards those goals. He shared of his success in business, but also that God had blessed him and his family—and could give them peace at that time.

Later Cliff excitedly called me to relay this story. I was saddened by the news but could not get over how his offering of speaking had been delayed by the Lord for His sovereign timing. It was as if we had a glimpse of God's hand in this troubled population. I call that my "roll-back-heaven story."

"Do everything without complaining or arguing, so that you may become blameless and pure, children of God without fault in a crooked and depraved generation, in which you shine like stars in the universe as you hold out the word of life—in order

that I may boast on the day of Christ that I did not run or labor for nothing." Phil. 2:14-16

FOR FURTHER REFLECTING:

In this chapter I share of how I learned to recognize when God was nudging me to give something, something that was a "good fit" for just what the people needed at the school. One time it was fresh lilacs with a simple hand-made card. A few times it was to pray appropriately on campus. Once it was to relay a picture I'd seen in prayer about that person. What do you have in abundance that maybe you can share? Think about what you have in your yard or home or pantry that you might serve up or give to a worn-out counselor or principal or teacher.

_____

_____

_____

_____

_____

_____

_____

_____

_____

"A word fitly spoken is like apples of gold in a setting of silver" *(Prov. 25:11, ESV).*

Kris Richards

CHAPTER 9

CHURCHES COME ON BOARD

B esides our friend Cliff Chappell, other pastors became part of this prayer movement. A neighborhood pastor Kelly Cohoe noticed that kids from the school across the street were starting to hang out on the front porch of his church before school in the mornings. Instead of making them leave, he decided to make them happy. He started serving the George Middle School students hot chocolate. The youth loved it, and began enjoying hanging out on the church's porch. The youth pastor brought out games in the sunshine for them to play. This continued for quite some time. For whatever reason, these kids from the at-risk feeder school to Roosevelt were coming to school early, thereby building relationship with Grace Community Church. Pastor Kelly, just like Pastor Cliff Chappell with the Spanish class at the high school, recognized an opportunity to serve as God opened the doors.

Other pastors began to respond to God's nudges as well for the schools in the Roosevelt neighborhood. In a nearby restaurant, a frustrated principal noticed a couple pastors from Mt. Olivet Church, a popular black church with a positive presence in the community. The principal approached the pastors. "Do you mind if we meet with you? Our school has so many kids with absent fathers. Your church has pillars in this community. Can we talk about partnering?" What these men didn't know is that the youth pastor of Mt. Olivet, Omari Jones, had been praying for months for a way to help this notorious school. He wanted to start up a prayer covering, but felt that relationship needed to be established first.

Leaders from the church and the school met at the school office. The administrators voiced desperate and humble requests for assistance in practical ways. They needed big men to just stand in the cafeteria at lunchtime to help maintain order. They wanted folks to "adopt" their single moms to help their kids with those extra reports when the moms are working long days and cannot help with homework. They also yearned for someone to take some of the single-parent students under their wing at school events. Everything the principal asked for he got--and then some--as the church leadership decided that the church members were to pour their hearts into partnering with the school—no strings attached. I remember Omari calling me after this meeting, excitedly sharing of the favor opening up with Portsmouth Middle School. This was the break-through that Omari had been praying for!

Across town, I decided to stop at a McDonalds where I never eat. I was in the vicinity for a doctor's appointment and thought I'd stop for my son to play on the climbing structure. As I watched my toddler play, I noticed an African American family seated also out in the play area. For some reason, my eye was drawn to this family. Were they Christians? They bowed their heads to pray. A conversation ensued that I'll never forget.

This man was a Christian. In fact, Greg Johnson was a pastor from Mt. Olivet Church, who was aiming to plant a branch of the church in the Caucasian neighborhoods of nearby Beaverton. Greg also rarely went to that McDonalds. I began to tell him my story and association with Mt. Olivet in North Portland. Greg listened intently. "This is amazing! Just today while driving over here I was gripping the steering wheel extra hard and crying out, 'God! Show us how to reach this high school where we meet! We need a break-through!'"

God was obviously at work! Greg called some of his elders on the car ride home from McDonalds. Later, he asked if my family and I could come to their church and join them in their monthly prayer walk. A few weeks later, we spoke in the gym of Sunset High School where this new church was meeting. As we walked the halls and prayed after church, one person got the idea of helping to clean up the school. They ran with that idea for several months. It was later reported in the news that this church and a few others became responsible for saving the district $30,000 in janitorial fees!

Each of these churches responded differently to the needs of their local school. It eventually did lead to a prayer covering as relationships were built. At each church, the leadership looked at real needs or real circumstances and did something to address them. It was a win-win situation, and God got the glory.

Later, this church's example and others became catalysts for other churches choosing to serve in something called a "Season of Service" of local churches meeting real needs in local schools. (See appendix for article on this.)

FOR FURTHER REFLECTING:

Sometimes churches decide their outreaches based on opinions of people inside the church. What if we instead chose our outreach based on what people were asking for outside the church—in our nearby school? The story relayed in this chapter was part of a huge movement God was doing in Portland that is now a model replicated across our country. Sometimes it was as easy as allowing a school staff to use church parking spaces due to lack of parking in an urban school setting. Talk to your church leadership about sitting down with your nearby school and asking if there's anything your church body can meet in terms of felt needs. Make a list of felt needs that the school makes known. Pray about how your church might shoulder those needs.

_____
_____
_____
_____
_____
_____
_____
_____
_____

"And whoever in the name of a disciple gives to one of these little ones even a cup of cold water to drink, truly I say to you, he shall not lose his reward" (Matt 10:42).

CHAPTER 10

"SURE, I CAN DO THAT!"

Remember Dorothy's famous line from *Wizard of Oz*? "Toto, I don't think we are not in Kansas anymore." That could have become my motto as I jumped into serving at Roosevelt High. I found myself in unfamiliar territory on more than one occasion. Like a runner in a relay race, I kept going forward.

The second year into this prayer covering, I was no longer living in the neighborhood. Our family had moved a half-hour north into Vancouver so our son could attend kindergarten at a Christian school where I taught part-time. In September while driving by Roosevelt during a football game, I prayed a quick prayer that it would do better in sports than it had for a very long time.

In November, I wandered into the SUN Schools office at Roosevelt High, which is a partnership of a government agency and Portland Public Schools to help meet the needs of the poorest students. While waiting to speak to Rebecca Green, the director, I took note of the others waiting to be helped. There was a pregnant Hispanic mother who was picking up bus tickets for her son. Another woman stood at the counter, shifting restlessly. She was trying to get help with a utilities bill after moving back into town. I found out they had moved three times back and forth to the coast in the last two years. As she talked, I noticed that most of her teeth were rotting. *Meth mouth,* I said to myself, recognizing its marks from previous exposure when I ran a ministry for the needy. I silently prayed that this time the mother would stay, and that her son would be able to finish school. A young pregnant woman was there with a teenage boy. I chatted with her and found they were coming for clothing. I asked her if she was the big sister of this boy. "No, I'm his step-mother," the woman said. I tried to hide my shock. This girl looked to be *maybe* 21, and she was raising a teenager!?

"So you want to help us. Do you *really* want to help us?" asked Rebecca in a cynical tone. She had been burned by churches promising to partner who had pulled out when they found out they couldn't press people to join their church.

"Yes, I'm willing to help. No strings attached." Rebecca and I had a long conversation about generational poverty, and I added to my growing knowledge I had gained from helping at a local food bank a few years before. I listened carefully, purposing to not be another church turning its back on the poor—for her sake as well as theirs. Rebecca became a teacher to this teacher, who was now choosing to be the student so I could learn all that I could. I found out that 37% of the students at Roosevelt were technically homeless. This meant that they lived on a grandparent's couch, or at the YWCA, or in a family car.

Below the school was a health clinic, and next to that, the Clothing Closet. This was a large room with used clothes for the homeless families, including younger siblings. Rebecca stated that they needed clothing donations.

"I can do something about that!" I told Rebecca,

immediately thinking of the moms group I helped run.

"I also have a bunch of kids who cannot afford to buy gifts for their families at Christmas. Could you bring in people to help teach crafts that would enable these kids to have something to give?" I thought of my artistic friend, Jana, who was always painting little cards and bookmarks.

"Sure, I think we can do that."

Then she told me of other ways to help: Round up professionals of color to come speak in classrooms about their trade and set up mentors to provide one-on-one help for seniors applying to college.

Within a month, friends from church had met or at least provided people to meet all four of these needs. The sixth grade class I was now teaching liked the idea of gathering clothing. They held a clothing drive at school. One compassionate student brought in two to three large bags full of clothing through donations from her church. The ladies who ran the Clothing Closet were starting to smile when I'd walk in the door, arms full of more clothing. Friends in my moms group would stop by the high school, babies in arms, and drop off bags of clothes. A dozen black friends from church offered to be one-time guest speakers for any teacher, which met the specific request from the SUN school director. A single friend with extra time on her hands signed up for the mentor training. Christians were responding!

Though we were batting a thousand in meeting each type of need, I knew we were just scratching the surface. Rebecca did tell me that there was a new hope in the students. "For them to know that many people out in the community are praying for them and are helping out… they know they aren't alone here anymore."

Change was becoming evident not only by the students, but even the substitute teachers. Here is a report from a sub teacher friend of mine.

> There is something different about substitute teaching at Roosevelt High.... I believe it is the Spirit of the Lord.
>
> There are now several AP (Advanced Placement) classes. I have subbed in those myself. Those kids in AP are motivated, eager, sociable in a good way and see a brighter future for themselves. Many students proudly wear sweatshirts with the RHS emblem. Now knowing this is the school where the prayer canopy started, I can attest without a doubt that the Spirit of the Lord is in that school. I could feel it from my first meeting of the students. I'm sure there are problems. However, the presence of the Lord is strong. There could almost be a revival if the walls could be torn down. After a day of service, I mentioned to a secretary and administrator, "there is something different about this high school compared to any other in the PPS system. I'm a veteran sub and I feel I can state this boldly." They were beaming from ear to ear along with me.
>
> Elaine Kempenich, substitute teacher, Portland Public Schools

THE DREAM: Around this time, I had a dream. I was standing inside Roosevelt High School, on brown carpet on the stairwell, looking out the window. I noticed that the carpet was new, and as I looked out, I saw hundreds of people all over the grounds.

"What's going on?" I asked a student in my dream.

"Don't you know? This school is being transformed." I looked closely. People were painting parts of the building. They were planting flowers and putting in beauty bark. Some kind of machinery like a steam roller was being used to put in a new surface beyond the grass.

I woke up and concluded that the dream must be symbolic of all the changes at the school from the prayers going up.

I kept doing what I'd been doing: teaching school, raising our boys, praying for Roosevelt, and occasionally stopping by the school to see what God was up to.

One sunny day in spring, I stopped in to drop off clothing. I noticed a television station van parked on the grass with a satellite dish raised high. I poked my head in at the office.

"What's going on?" I asked Connie, the secretary who by now was quite friendly with me.

"It's the boys' basketball team. They made it to state. There's a send-off party for them this afternoon."

I was ecstatic. "Can anybody come?"

"Sure!"

I wanted them to know we had their backs.

I called up my youth pastor friend, Omari Jones. "Omari! Can you make it to the school today at four? There's a send-off party for the boys' basketball team." I ran home and quickly penned a sign on fluorescent tag board. It said, "Local Churches Love RHS. We got your back covered!"

When I showed up at the school, I sadly found very few parents, about 50 students and a few teachers. Omari was there, balancing his toddler on his shoulders.

I will never forget what happened next. It was like the climax of a great movie. The double doors burst open to the vintage brick school building. Out ran every one of the young men on the basketball team. I didn't know any of them personally, but I felt like a proud mama as I held out my hand and "high-fived" every one of them, speaking encouraging words to each one.

After the team left, the principals were trying to hand out ice cream sandwiches to the remaining students. As they struggled to get them out of the box, I stepped in to help. It dawned on me that I had changed. I had gone from coming to Roosevelt because I wanted a job, to not caring about pay and reaping far greater rewards. I had shifted from thinking of what I could get from this school, to looking at the myriad of needs the school had and seeing how I might help meet them.

Could God be nudging you to do the same?

The Boys Basketball Team Honored in the Parade

Later the TV and newspapers would report that it was the first time in 53 years that Roosevelt High would make it to state. The basketball team took 2nd place that weekend, and garnered the "Best Sportsmanship" award of the tournament. God is *for* Roosevelt High School! Though the whole community may not be, though all the parents may not be, God is for these underdog schools!!

The day before Mother's Day was the annual St. Johns Parade. I sat with my two little boys and husband in folding chairs with hundreds of other spectators along the route. "And here's the Roosevelt Boys Basketball Team, just returned from State!" the announcer called out. I lost all composure. Like Sandra Bullock in *Blindside*, I bolted out of my seat, out of my comfort zone, jumping up and down for my team. That was my team!! The boys had no idea who I was, but I knew who they were. I had memorized their names while poring over the numerous newspaper articles.

In the two years that we had been praying and serving at Roosevelt, the press coverage of the school had gone from very negative to positive. Instead of only condemning articles coming out, there were shining ones. One story was titled, *"Roughriders Rising Tide: Basketball just Part of a Wave Lifting All Boats at Roosevelt."* Within a few months, I would have a file almost an inch thick of positive articles about Roosevelt High School. God was responding to our prayers!!

(See Appendices for articles about Roosevelt.)

FOR FURTHER REFLECTING:

When you look at the list you made last chapter of felt needs expressed from a local school, do any jump off the page at you as something you might do? I had that sense over and over in this chapter of "I can do that!" I may not have solved the problem, but I knew people who could. When we are rich with relational resources and we are looking at a school or student population needy in resources, it's not difficult to connect the dots. Talk to your home group, or moms group, or your own family about if or how you might be able to do one of those things on the list.

_____

_____

_____

_____

_____

_____

_____

_____

_____

_____

"Each one should use whatever gift he has received to serve others, faithfully administering God's grace in its various forms" (I Peter 4:10).

CHAPTER 11

"THIS NEEDS TO SPREAD ALL OVER THE DISTRICT!"

B y the end of the first year that we prayed, people were talking. One day late in the year I walked by the office of the head principal, Deborah Peterson. She pulled me inside in confidence. "Last year at this time we had 30 suspensions." Her voice rose excitedly. "This year we had only three!" I was shocked. That was a 90% reduction! God was answering our prayers!

Another time I met a new assistant principal at Roosevelt. He told me that half-way through the year, the district had removed the previous assistant principal. She was giving away an average of four referrals (punishing students by sending them home) per day. This new assistant principal? One referral a *week*. That is a significant improvement!

In the summer time, the St. Johns Business Association had its quarterly meeting. It was an "open-mic" time when anyone could stand up and share what they'd been seeing in their business or in St. Johns. After a while, everyone began asking, "WHAT happened at Roosevelt High this year?" Everyone was astonished by the reduction of behavior problems and by the turn-around coverage in the newspaper. One woman in the audience, Cathy Cunningham, sat listening as person after person remarked about all the improvements at Roosevelt over the year. Finally, Cathy, whose husband was a pastor of a local church and had been part of our prayer canopy, excitedly took her turn at the mic.

"You want to know why things changed at Roosevelt this year? I'll tell you why! A bunch of people all over North Portland decided to pray for every student and teacher there weekly--all year."

Cathy later told me that you could hear a pin drop after her remarks. Whether or not the business community wanted to acknowledge it, God had been behind the changes for the better!

That August, Deborah Petersen sent a letter out to the community from the office of Roosevelt High School. It was a memo itemizing specific ways how the school had turned around in the last year—her first year as principal. (See appendix for this memo.) She specifically thanked the community for its involvement in helping support Roosevelt that past year. The specifics listed?

- 85% reduction in all behavior problems
- 10% gain across the departments of the school in the Oregon state standardized tests.
- Highest test-score gains of the 15 high school in Portland Public Schools.
- Lowest graffiti rate in the district

- Parent participation up to 83% who showed up at the back-to-school meeting

The results of this memo were so staggering that a year later we were flown out to Oahu to speak to pastors and intercessors who had started up the original Hawaii prayer canopy. Some of the people had grown weary from the school prayer movement they'd started up a few years earlier, and they needed encouragement to stick with it.

Our friend and mentor Pastor Cal Chinen asked me to speak to Christian educators and the praying community about what God did in Portland. My heart was full—like Peter's in Acts when he proclaimed, "I cannot help but speak of what I have seen or heard." I was nervous to speak, as the keynote speaker was Argentine evangelist Ed Silvoso, whose prayer-walking model had inspired Cal's son Daniel when he visited Argentina a few years earlier. A huge highlight of that weekend speaking was meeting Daniel, who courageously brought the baton of this prayer movement to Hawaii to begin with!

After I spoke, I asked Cal how I did in addressing the pastors. I was so nervous and didn't feel super polished. "Kris, you hit the ball out of the park!" Cal told me. The news of what God did at Roosevelt High was just what the pastors on Oahu needed to hear.

They will tell of the power of your awesome works, and I will proclaim your great deeds. Psalm 145:6

That Sunday in Kaneohe, Ralph Moore, pastor of New Hope Winward church, asked me to speak. Ralph had grown up in Portland and vividly remembered Roosevelt's notoriety. He asked me to share about the good things God had done in our two years of praying for Roosevelt. So earnest was he to get the Roosevelt story out that he photocopied the memo I'd received from the principal and placed it on every chair of his large church. Then he videotaped us relaying the story at the Friday night service and showed it to all five of his weekend services! God is good! He is faithful!

In Spring of 2007, the principal of Roosevelt was working with a math teacher to implement a homework policy that would give incentives from community businesses for kids who got all their homework in. Here is an email from then-principal Deborah Peterson.

Deborah Peterson (dpeterso@pps.k12.or.us)
6/27/07

Dear Friends, thank you so much for your consideration of this effort. Your support has been so amazing the past two years and has made the difference with our progress. We can only do this work because of your support! -Deborah

Deborah Peterson, Campus Principal, Roosevelt High School Campus

Here is more feedback I received:

From my friend starting the prayer canopy an hour south of Portland in Albany, Oregon:
8/08/07

> YEAH!!! God is so good to His kids. I am so excited for you guys [up in North Portland]. Good stuff happening here [in Albany, OR] too. I met a lady last night who is a teacher in Lebanon [Oregon]. They have

been praying for the schools there and are going to be praying about doing it there.

September 2nd is the night we are going to light up West Albany High...PRAISE THE LORD! The doors are wide open with the school principal and we have her blessing to pray over the school and the kids. I really feel like this is huge!

Kathy :)

The following emails are from Portland Police Officer Bob Tallman, the officer assigned to Parkrose High School and Middle Schools, about ten miles east of Roosevelt. Bob wrote to me about the changes he noticed after the first year praying and then two years later. Bob is a Christian who was favorable of our prayer.

Feb. 13, 2008

Hi Kris and Jennifer [Jennifer was the mom who started the prayer canopy at Parkrose].

Thx for praying. The past couple months the big stuff either seemed to subside or get exposed early for intervention (i.e. gang issues, pending fights, etc). I started to be amazed at when we did have stuff come up, kids were open about what was going on. That's a praise. Overall, the district feels more peaceful.

(After two years of prior praying, Bob wrote the following email January 18, 2010):

75

Prayer has been effective...here are a few examples this year...

- *Overall, things have been calmer. (There is a more positive perception of the community).*
- *Racial tension has lessened & kids of different races seem to be interacting more. Parkrose has rapidly become international with about 32 language groups.*
- *The gang problem at the high school and middle school has been minimal. (Parkrose has become a sort of quiet zone in the city for gang activity...a huge change from what we were dealing with previously.)*
- *The rash of constant medical emergencies we used to have has significantly dropped.*
- *The sports teams at the high school started rebounding (I know some prayed for this).*

Remember the police officer at Roosevelt High who said if things improved he would join our prayer movement? Well, he ended up becoming one of our biggest advocates. At the end of the first school year he told me, "Almost all gang activity is gone here. We are dealing with things like skipping class and smoking. This {prayer canopy} should be allowed at every school in Portland!"

The next year, I poked my head in his office to say hi. He was in a meeting with a parent, but he stood up despite the meeting and proclaimed, *"Do you realize that if this continues, I could be out of a job?! Things are still improving here! This needs to happen all over this school district!"*

Obviously, God was spreading this way beyond Roosevelt High.

FOR FURTHER REFLECTING:

This chapter shares good reports, or great news of what can happen as God moves on hearts and brings results. Think of a good report that has happened at the place or school where you have been praying. Is this good news actually a result of a specific prayer you or someone on your prayer team asked God for? Don't be surprised if you see the results of your prayers—or become the results!

_____

_____

_____

_____

_____

_____

_____

_____

_____

_____

_____

"If you abide in me, and My words abide in you, ask whatever you wish, and it will be done for you." John 15:7 (NASB)

Kris Richards

CHAPTER 12

THE BIG PICTURE

My manila envelope with newspaper clippings about Roosevelt High was now an inch thick. They were all positive articles about this notorious high school. One day, I sat down to read one such article in The *Oregonian*. Much of the shift was when the school decided to hire Frank Chisman to take on fundraising. Frank chose to leave one of the prestigious Catholic schools in town to promote Roosevelt High. With funding cuts, there was no band, no choir, or drama department. I remember attending a St. Johns parade. Three former members of the band soberly marched by, carrying a banner, "Roosevelt Band: R.I.P."

The wealthier schools had strong PTA's that could dig deep and come up with money for instruments or for an after-school band. Parents at those schools could handle a $60 "user fee" for their kids to be in sports or clubs. Not at Roosevelt. Frank was quoted as "feeling called to this school." From our new home in Vancouver, I read the article and cheered aloud.

Marty Jackson, a dad of a boy on the baseball team, helped run the booster club, garnering funds from his popular sandwich shop. Marty ended up working with Frank, business leaders and alumni interested in supporting the booster club. These men rallied the community to renew the tradition of "tail gate parties" before the football games.

The biggest tailgate party was at the homecoming football game. Nike ™ had donated the complete turf to lay a new field as well as track. Steam rollers came out to lay the surface, just like I'd seen in my dream. Parents and the community were there in force. Mayor Sam Adams was present to flip the game coin, and various dignitaries from the city were there to see all the changes at Roosevelt. A local TV station's helicopter landed beside the field for radio coverage of the game.

In the summer of 2007, just a few months earlier, our family was driving to the coast for the weekend. I will never forget what we heard on the local news while snaking out of Portland on the Sunset Highway. A thousand volunteers from Southlake Church had decided to give a day serving Roosevelt by cleaning and beautifying it, inside and out. I grabbed my husband's arm and called out in disbelief, tears streaming down my face. "This is just what I saw in my dream!" We were ecstatic. This clean-up day was the kick-off to the Season of Service, a city-wide effort by churches to serve in the local community.

Later that summer, evangelist Luis Palau filled the Waterfront Park with 30,000 people. They came to hear popular singers like Toby Mac and Curtis Wilson. Stunt skateboarders defied gravity on huge pipes and bars set up before the crowd. As a spectator in the audience, I was moved when they introduced the Summer of Service. A video was projected on the giant screen of the crowds of people who had come to Roosevelt High School to clean up the campus. It was the footage from the radio coverage I'd heard while driving to the coast. Church members had planted trees, spread beauty bark, and painted—saving the school district thousands of dollars. This became a pattern of churches helping schools throughout the city that summer— and a model now replicated across the nation.

The video, filmed by the Luis Palau Association, later became part of a documentary. The very scenes from my dream are in that film! The one-hour movie is called "Undivided." http://www.undividedthemovie.com/ Southlake Church provided the majority of the volunteers for that Day of Service. Situated in affluent West Linn, this church decided to do something about the disparity between the wealthy schools where they lived and the poorer schools like Roosevelt High. They also met with school administrators and asked how they could help. Says senior pastor Kip Jacob from Southlake in an article on CBN News, "Evangelism usually connotes words. And so this is more about works. Rather than proclamation only, it's more about demonstration. And really about demonstrating good news, which we think ultimately is what changes people's lives. (CBN News 22 Feb, 2015).

How did all this happen? How did Southlake Church get such a burden for Roosevelt High? I believe that their involvement flowed out of the prayers of our little group of 60 intercessors who'd been praying—and serving--the two years' prior.

The story goes back further. At one point I was invited to attend the area-wide meeting of Moms in Touch, the international prayer movement that challenges PTA moms to pray for each child in her son's or daughter's class. "I believe the changes at Roosevelt High are a result of prayer

81

from people who decided to not ignore this high school," I told the hundreds of women who packed out the hotel banquet room in SE Portland. "But the movement that we started is a direct answer to the prayers of two women in your group who dared to ask God for this—every week they met—in 2004. We are the answer to your prayers! Thank you for caring for North Portland and for that overlooked high school called Roosevelt. It is no longer forgotten." [1]

A year after this film was made, a North Portland paper ran a story about crime in the area. The new police chief, Susie Sizemore, had moved around the top brass in Portland. It seems that crime had gone up in all parts of the city *except* North Portland. They did not need as many police officers on duty in St. Johns anymore and were moving them to other precincts. Was that from the little army of intercessors? Perhaps. Did Southlake Church hear of what we had done? Eventually. All I can say is *God did* these things.

- God nudged two ladies with Moms in Touch (now called Moms in Prayer, International—Momsinprayer.org) to pray for a whole year for a mom in St. Johns to get a burden for Roosevelt High School and its feeder schools.
- God caused me to run into pastors and to get the Word of the Lord from Loren Cunningham with my husband, setting in motion a whole series of events that would lead us to bring this prayer canopy to Oregon.
- God turned around Roosevelt High School and continues to do so today as Southlake Church continues to serve there.

---

[1] An interesting side-note we discovered is that Moms in Prayer was started by Fern Nichols, who attended Roosevelt High School!

- God is now telling this story not only through the movie, but across the country. *The New York Times* ran an online article about Roosevelt High and Southlake Church in August of 2013. (http://www.nytimes.com/2013/08/10/us/help-from-evangelicals-without-the-evangelizing.html?_r=0)
- CBN covered the story in February, 2015 (http://www1.cbn.com/cbnnews/us/2015/February/School-Transformed-after-Church-Gives-Up-Right-to-Preach)

Four years later after our prayer canopy was launched, there was a meeting of 500 public school officials and pastors from the greater Portland area. They were sitting at many round tables, talking of needs, and seeing how they can meet them. There is now a website called Project City Serve (Songreaterportland.ning.com) where people all over the city can click on a school and find out what practical needs they have. There is a contact person from the school where a family, Bible study, or youth group can find out how they, too, can pick up the baton.

Or, they can go to http://www.undividedthemovie.com/ and click on "Every school matters."

FOR FURTHER REFLECTING:

It's so amazing how God sets things in motion. Like some kind of cosmic chess board, one thing happens that becomes the set-up for another thing. Think of a time you realized you got to play a part in a much bigger thing God had been up to. Recall what that was, and what led to what in terms of more fruitfulness?

_____

_____

_____

_____

_____

_____

_____

_____

_____

_____

_____

_____

I planted the seed, Apollos watered it, but God has been making it grow. I Cor. 3:6

CHAPTER 13

LESSONS LEARNED ALONG THE WAY

In praying and serving our way through the exciting changes in the Roosevelt High story, we learned some solid lessons. As I alluded to earlier, God provided unexpected "teachers" along the way.

Parent and sandwich shop owner Marty Jackson taught me to not give up on my local high school. He was one of the few Christian parents who did not leave for the suburbs, and who worked alongside his son all four years there. Marty is the one early-on who told my husband and me:

"As the local high school goes, so goes the community."

Those words riveted my heart. Here was a guy who probably could have afforded to drive his son to one of the more prestigious high schools in the West Hills. But he didn't. He encouraged his son to try out for baseball. Then he became the assistant coach, leading the team in prayer before the games. When his son went out for basketball, Marty was cheering him on all the way to state. As the football team was turning around its losing streak, Marty was turning around the fan base by stirring up the tailgate parties of parents in the parking lot.

Another mentor to this educator was the director of the SUN Schools office, Rebecca Green. Rebecca had a cynical attitude about people from local churches coming to help at her school--for due cause. She saw strings attached to assistance, such as a requirement that dollars given would mean the people would have to attend a certain church. I assured her that people truly compelled by love would not put that on others. Jesus gave unconditionally, and so should we. If we offer something practical and then make it contingent on their darkening our doorways, we are no better than savvy business people trying to gain a new lead for a sale. Slowly, Rebecca came to realize that we truly were in it for the long-term.

This isn't a business deal. These are individual children who are overlooked and who need to be cared for. These are teachers who are in the trenches, slugging it out day after day with an ability range that would be staggering for even a team of teachers to take on.

Deborah Peterson, the former principal, was an invaluable advocate for the youth at Roosevelt High. The dictionary defines one who "intercedes" as one who makes entreaty on behalf of another. She was that, a go-betweener. While we were going-between earth and heaven with our prayers for Roosevelt High, Deborah would bridge the gap daily between the parents who had never finished high school and their son or daughter who was determined to go to college. She would march down that center path that cut the front lawn in half and would chase gangsters off of her campus when they'd pull up in cars crammed with young men. This was her school. "Not on *my* watch," her actions would shout.

I used to teach at an at-risk school prior to having children. I thought I was pretty committed if I spent a half hour on the phone with a parent who needed insight on their child. Deborah's commitment level way overshadowed mine. She related to me once how she drove seven hours to Washington State University and literally took a boy from his gangster friends in St. Johns and handed him off to the officials for on-campus housing and registration at WSU. She'd do anything to pioneer a new path for the kids of Roosevelt High School. Deborah is a big part of their story, and eventually became one of our quiet advocates.

"Do you realize," she told me five years after we began praying, "that everything started to turn around when you people started praying?" I couldn't believe my ears. This was the woman who in the spring of 2006 contended that "we worked hard" was the reason for the dramatic turn-around. My countering with, "And we prayed" seemed to fall on deaf ears.   But not five years later.   She admitted to me the following improvements of her school:

- Roosevelt went from zero advanced placement (A.P.) classes to eight.
- Southlake Church got involved and cleaned up the campus during the summers, saving thousands of dollars.
- Roosevelt had made it to state in basketball, made it to the playoffs in soccer, and actually saw some "W's" on the scoreboard in football.
- Roosevelt's Spanish teacher got Oregon Teacher of the Year

After reflecting on these "teachers" who educated this educator, I did some soul-searching. We had planned to keep our sons in a Christian school for their education. How could I have a completely separationist point of view as a

87

fellow Christian? Should I not at least consider putting my sons in a public high school? As I write this, our older son is in 8th grade. We are continuing these prayer walks now in Kona, Hawaii. Perhaps because of Marty Jackson's words eight years ago, I am planning on putting our son Evan at Kealakehe High School for his freshman year. I saw from Marty's involvement that a child in a local school does not mean only the child is in that school: so are the parents!

The Bible teaches there is wisdom in many counselors. I want to heed the words and the modeling of these "counselors," and carry forward what they taught me. Like Deborah Petersen, I want to be a bridge-builder to the schools.

FOR FURTHER REFLECTING:

Deborah Petersen had this inner resolve to protect her boys from being sucked into the local gangs. She was the principal of that school and was the God-placed authority there. When she chased those guys off the campus, they went far away! What is a place where God has placed you that you know you have some authority? What are the dreams or ways you are contending for to protect that place or people?

_____

_____

_____

_____

_____

_____

_____

_____

_____

_____

In Nehemiah 2:4, The king asks his cupbearer Nehemiah, "What is it you want?" Nehemiah feels to ask his employer to be released to go rebuild the wall. The king gives him favor: a horse, soldiers, letters to cross the adjacent land, etc. Perhaps God has given you a burden for a place or people and is asking you what you fully want for that place?

Kris Richards

CHAPTER 14

STARTING YOUR OWN PRAYER CANOPY

I recently read the best-selling book *The Tipping Point* by Malcolm Gladwell. I'm curious to know how different events in history have brought change across a whole region or nation. It's fascinating stuff. All massive movements have had "connectors," or people who have friends across many segments of society. They aren't locked into a narrow, homogenous group. They move across sectors and they flip information across those sectors.

I want to be that type of person. Perhaps I can connect with you—to hand the baton off—so that you can run. It's not a long thing, just your leg of this journey for the school in your community. As I've shared this simple model at women's retreats or casually with friends, moms have seen that it's *doable*. Many have started a prayer canopy in some form or another over their local school.

In the book of Revelation, John talks about the prayers of the saints going up like incense to the Lord (Revelation 5:8). John later speaks of the bowl that tips at a certain point, bringing down fire and power to the earth (Revelation 8:3-5).

91

I don't understand that. But I think that's a bit of what we've seen at Roosevelt High. God heard us. He gave us what we asked for.

"If you abide in me, and my Word abides in you, ask what you will, and it shall be done unto you." John 15:7

Prayers have continued on a regular basis, with blessings being spoken out over these schools. Something has shifted. Statistics have changed. Annual behavior reports on state websites have gone from dismal to better.

WHAT WE DID:

*We were honest** with the school leadership. We told them that we were going to pray—on our own, all year long, for their school to improve. We were there to bless their school, not to build our church numbers or to evangelize their campus.

*We sought input** of specific ways they wanted to see things improve. We asked those on the inside what they would like to see happen at their school. They know best what is needed.

*We mobilized praying people** using public- access information—first names from the school yearbooks.

*We kept it simple**. It was finding out who the people were who were willing to pray—once a week all year long—and giving them ten names each on little cards we ran off, until the whole school was covered. At Roosevelt High this was a handful of moms, three to four churches—and praying folks at those churches. The next year when it started at other schools, I took cards from those schools and gave them to teachers and students of the Christian school where I taught. In my sixth grade class, we stopped every Thursday morning and took a few minutes to pray for the ten names on our cards. Within a few weeks, we had the names memorized. (See appendix for the form we created.)

On each prayer card, we listed the names of nine students and one staff. *Note: freshmen will not be in the last year's yearbook, so you will need to see if an administrator can get you their first names.* We listed the names on one side and two to four ways of how they can pray on the back, based on what the principal or school officer told us they wanted to see happen. I always added one other prayer need to the list: "for students to be drawn to things of God."

***We stayed in touch.** This went both ways. We let our praying folks know when things were improving—or getting worse, and we stayed in touch with our person on the inside.

***We prayer walked when needed.** When we would hear of a downturn from our contact on the inside, we would gather our intercessors to pray and walk. It wasn't during school, but on a weekend when we all could meet. The prayer walk lasted an hour max and looked like people in two's and three's walking around talking with each other. Nothing dramatic. We did this when we heard of drugs on the rise, or a gang that was forming, or a trend of students hurting themselves. And we saw results! God heard our prayers and tipped the scales!

WANT TO START THIS UP IN YOUR COMMUNITY?

1) Begin by praying. (See addendum for suggested format.)

2) Ask the school leaders what are their needs.

3) As God leads and puts the burdens on people's hearts, allow them to come alongside you and serve to help meet those specific needs.

4) Keep praying as God leads you in how to pray and serve!

WHAT ABOUT SHARING THE LORD?

What I found was that people became hungry for God through the results of our praying. School staff was astounded: first that anyone cared enough to do this and second that they saw results. Some wanted to commend me for this. I always told them it was God answering the prayers. We just knew enough to go to Him in the first place. I also gently offered that they could go to Him as well. We were not some magic conduit.

Through the relationships and trust built from these prayer canopies, we saw doors flung open for service. Some of us picked up that baton, and would find that we became the answer to our own prayers. We saw friendships forged with teachers and administrators. When something went down at the school, we would be there. We could hug the teacher crying after her student took his life, or could pray with the teacher on the phone as she realized her daughter was almost in the fatal car wreck. As principals came to see that we weren't a bunch of gossipers but folks who truly cared, they would confide in us of continued ways to pray. Doubters in prayer became pleasantly surprised by answers. Distant observers became friends. God did—and still does—a great thing as the baton passes from school to school.

THINGS I FIGURED OUT ALONG THE WAY:

Remember the story of Saul the reluctant leader? I spent much of my time not knowing what to do other than to *keep going*. I tried to do the little practical things as the Lord led me. Here are some of those things I did that you might want to try. Ask the Lord if there is a form of these that works for your setting.

*When I got the idea of picking lilacs and delivering them with a little card to the principal, I just found what was in my backyard, put it in a vase, and added beautiful writing to my "we have your back covered" card. What's in your backyard?

*When I stumbled upon the party for the boys' basketball team going to state, I saw principals needing help handing out stuff, so I handed out stuff. I will never forget hand-over-fisting ice cream sandwiches to hungry students at that celebration. The principal was on my left and an assistant principal was on my right. I just helped them accomplish what they were trying to do. Isn't that largely what this is all about?

*At that spring baseball game when I handed out strawberries, I don't know why I bought strawberries. They were in season! God put that on my heart. I just picked up a few tubs and distributed them to the few people in the stands that day at the game. Those simple fruits led to introductions with key people. Maybe that will happen for you.

*Remember the poppy lapels? I just saw that the secretary was trying to sell something for the students. I bought one poppy pin for a few bucks and proudly wore it. It showed the teachers that I was with them. It didn't really matter what the fundraiser was, but I invested a little bit and was alongside them in helping those kids. They saw that, and it made a difference.

Sporting the poppy label as I play with our younger son, Josiah

WHAT ABOUT THOSE OPPORTUNITIES TO SPEAK?

I often feel like Peter as I've quoted before: **"I cannot help speak of what I have seen and heard."** Or David when he says, **"I will sing your praises. I will not be silent" (Psalm 30:12).**

When God starts moving, we get to point out what great things He is doing. He gets the glory! The school improves. Principals and teachers are happy. They come out on top… and the students benefit. Who knows the end of what God can do when we ask for it on behalf of these hurting schools? Whether it's a turn-around in sports, tests scores improving, or parent participation on the rise. It might be fights down or a school police officer telling you gang activity is gone.

On the other hand, God might not give you a word for a school principal. You may not hear answers to your dreams on the radio, or in scenes in a movie. But as one mom to another, I can tell you when you pray for your local school and listen to God's promptings, It can become a wild ride that goes way beyond what you can imagine.

You may be grabbing that baton and hanging on for a while.

"Now to Him who is able to do far more abundantly beyond all that we ask or think, according to the power that works within us, to Him be the glory in the church and in Christ Jesus to all generations forever and ever. Amen." Ephesians 3:20-21 (NASB)

Kris Richards

98

APPENDICES

APPENDIX 1
(MEMO FROM THE PRINCIPAL AFTER OUR
YEAR OF PRAYING-- AUG. 25, 2006)

CONGRATULATIONS!

Roosevelt
made the biggest gains
of all the high schools
in Portland Public Schools!

- BIGGEST gains in TEST SCORES!
- Parent involvement at Report Card Night at 82%!
- Decrease of discipline issues up to 85%!
- Biggest reduction of vandalism of all Portland High Schools!

Thank you to our students, families, North Portland Community Partners, Boosters, neighbors, teachers, and staff! When we work together as a team of educators, students, families, and community members, WE CAN MAKE A DIFFERENCE IN THE LIVES OF OUR KIDS!!!!

SPRING 2006 Achievement Results

ACT	04-05	05-06	GAIN
READING	24.6%	36.4%	+11.8%
MATH	11.7%	27.3%	+15.6%
SCIENCE	19.7%	48.5%	+28.8%
WRITING	38.6%	46.2%	+7.6%

POWER	04-05	05-06	GAIN
READING	15.6%	24.6%	+9%
MATH	9.8%	20.3%	+10.5%
SCIENCE	12.8%	37.9%	+25.1%
WRITING	24.3%	35.4%	+11.1%

SEIS	04-05	05-06	GAIN
READING	24.4%	27.1%	+2.7%
MATH	18.2%	36.0%	+17.8%
SCIENCE	21.4%	33.3%	+11.9%
WRITING	36.6%	33.3%	-3.3%

ACT = Arts, Communication and Technology (at Roosevelt High School)
POWER = Pursuit of WELLNESS EDUCATION (at Roosevelt High School)
SEIS = Spanish English International School (at Roosevelt High School)

RHS grads that get college gradu at a higher than any oth high school.

C:\desktop\data\data results for community 8-25-06.doc

APPENDIX 2A
(PRAYER CARDS SIDE A)

<table>
<tr>
<td>

PRAY WEEKLY FOR
_____
HIGH SCHOOL

1.
2.
3.
4.
5.
6.
7.
8.
9.
Staff:

</td>
<td>

PRAY WEEKLY FOR
_____
HIGH SCHOOL

1.
2.
3.
4.
5.
6.
7.
8.
9.
Staff:

</td>
<td>

PRAY WEEKLY FOR
_____
HIGH SCHOOL

1.
2.
3.
4.
5.
6.
7.
8.
9.
Staff:

</td>
</tr>
<tr>
<td>

PRAY WEEKLY FOR
_____
HIGH SCHOOL

1.
2.
3.
4.
5.
6.
7.
8.
9.
Staff:

</td>
<td>

PRAY WEEKLY FOR
_____
HIGH SCHOOL

1.
2.
3.
4.
5.
6.
7.
8.
9.
Staff:

</td>
<td>

PRAY WEEKLY FOR
_____
HIGH SCHOOL

1.
2.
3.
4.
5.
6.
7.
8.
9.
Staff:

</td>
</tr>
</table>

APPENDIX 2B
(PRAYER CARDS SIDE B)

PORTLAND SCHOOLS
CANOPY OF PRAYER

PRAY EACH WEEK FOR:

*GENERAL BLESSING

*PROTECTION

*WISE DECISION MAKING

*HEARTS SOFTENED TO THINGS OF GOD

PORTLAND SCHOOLS
CANOPY OF PRAYER

PRAY EACH WEEK FOR:

*GENERAL BLESSING

*PROTECTION

*WISE DECISION MAKING

*HEARTS SOFTENED TO THINGS OF GOD

PORTLAND SCHOOLS
CANOPY OF PRAYER

PRAY EACH WEEK FOR:

*GENERAL BLESSING

*PROTECTION

*WISE DECISION MAKING

*HEARTS SOFTENED TO THINGS OF GOD

PORTLAND SCHOOLS
CANOPY OF PRAYER

PRAY EACH WEEK FOR:

*GENERAL BLESSING

*PROTECTION

*WISE DECISION MAKING

*HEARTS SOFTENED TO THINGS OF GOD

PORTLAND SCHOOLS
CANOPY OF PRAYER

PRAY EACH WEEK FOR:

*GENERAL BLESSING

*PROTECTION

*WISE DECISION MAKING

*HEARTS SOFTENED TO THINGS OF GOD

PORTLAND SCHOOLS
CANOPY OF PRAYER

PRAY EACH WEEK FOR:

*GENERAL BLESSING

*PROTECTION

*WISE DECISION MAKING

*HEARTS SOFTENED TO THINGS OF GOD

APPENDIX 4
(FROM *THE OREGONIAN* MARCH 8, 2009)

COMMENTARY ON ISSUES THAT MATTER IN THE NORTHWEST

Kristine Sommer (second from right) visits with volunteers and speakers before the start of last week's all-girls assembly at Roosevelt High School. Sommer is SouthLake Foursquare Church's on-site representative at the school, where she works to coordinate church volunteers assisting students.

FAITH CATHCART THE OREGONIAN

By TOM KRATTENMAKER

The Southlake Foursquare Church's on-site representative at the school, where Kristine Sommer works to coordinate volunteers assisting students.

APPENDIX 5
(FROM *THE OREGONIAN* MARCH 8, 2009)

The Oregonian paper details how churches are starting to form partnerships with local schools to serve at the schools in the "Season of Service."

APPENDIX 6
(FROM *THE OREGONIAN* OCT. 16, 2008)

Students and alumni from Roosevelt visiting the Portland City Council were invited to the Homecoming football game. Parents and community members re-kindled the old "tailgate parties" to woo in more boosters to the football program.

APPENDIX 7
(FROM *THE OREGONIAN* FEB. 19, 2009)

FOR THE LOVE OF THE PLAYERS

For one night, the stands were full and the playing field was level. For one night, the fans — "We have fans!" the Roosevelt girls were surely thinking — convinced a winless basketball team that it could do no wrong.

For one glorious night, the community laid hands on a high school that has been left by far too many for dead.

At the end of the loneliest of seasons, 1,600 cheerleaders packed the Roosevelt gym Tuesday for the Rough Riders' final home game, then spent two hours applauding Ahoefa Ananouko on the boards, Ericca Ducre on the break and Ilena Allen at the three-point arc.

When they had every reason to be intimidated, the girls were inspired,

STEVE DUIN

COMMENTARY

outscoring Madison 12-4 in the final quarter to lose by a single basket, 31-29. When asked what made the difference, Monique Carlson — the team's lone senior — said, "The support. Everyone was watching us. This is the most support we've ever had."

She wasn't nervous? Only when the entire gym stood and welcomed her to center court before the opening tip, Carlson said. "Then my hands started shaking and my stomach turning.

The rest of the time? "I knew that if I was personally nervous, the rest of the team would be nervous, too. Since I'm one of the captains, I have to pretend that everything is OK because everyone is looking up to me."

Please see **ROOSEVELT,** *Page A6*

STEPHANIE YAO LONG/THE OREGONIAN
Andrea Wujek (with sign) and Carly Koebel turn out with other members of the University of Portland women's basketball team to cheer Roosevelt.

To see a video and photo gallery from Tuesday night's Roosevelt High School girls basketball game, read Steve Duin's earlier column and share your opinion, go to **blog.oregonlive.com/steveduin**

Steve Duin writes for *The Oregonian* about the historic 1600 person turn-out to the girls' basketball game, the very thing we'd been asking God for in our prayer walk a few days beforehand! The on-line version of this article had comments from all over the city saying this was one of the most positive news stories people had read all year.

APPENDIX 8
(FROM *THE OREGONIAN* FEB. 8, 2009)

Crowd turns out to support Roughriders

In a carnival atmosphere, the Roosevelt girls lost their 18th consecutive basketball game Tuesday night ... and were celebrated every step of the way.

The Roughriders rewarded a capacity crowd of 1,600 with their best game of the season, before losing to the Madison Senators 31-29.

But the story of the night was the turnout of the community of Portland-area basketball fans. Teams from Putnam, West Linn, Clackamas and the University of Portland helped pack the Roosevelt gym in the Roughriders' final home game of the season.

Also on hand were several hundred supporters from SouthLake Foursquare Church of West Linn, which has a long-running commitment to the high school and the North Portland community.

Roosevelt (0-18, 0-11 Class 5A Portland Interscholastic League) was led in scoring by junior guard Ericca Ducre with seven points. Junior wing Rachel Rogers scored nine points to lead Madison (7-12, 6-4).

Roosevelt's lone senior, Monique Carlson, scored six points in her final home game.

—*Steve Duin*

Franklin clinches title: After seeing its winning streak stopped at eight games last week, Franklin couldn't lock up the Class 6A PIL ti-

OLIVIA BUCKS/THE OREGONIAN

An upset | Century's Cameron McCaffrey is fouled by Wilsonville's Seth Gearhart during the No. 8 Jaguars' 47-45 win over the No. 1 Wildcats.

Tualatin (15-6) held Tigard (18-5) to two points in the first quarter and outscored the Tigers 28-17 after halftime.

Kelly Millager scored 16 points for the Timberwolves, and Corinn Waltrip had 11 for Tigard.

Boys

Tight race in Northwest Oregon: Eighth-ranked Century took the lead with 20 seconds left and beat No. 1 Wilsonville 47-45 in Hillsboro to ratchet up the competitiveness at the top of the Northwest Oregon Conference standings.

Loren Langford's basket with 30 seconds left put Wilsonville (21-2, 10-2) ahead 45-44. Cameron McCaffrey answered for Century (16-6, 8-4) with a four-foot runner with 20 seconds remaining.

After the Wildcats missed a shot, Connor Cummings made one of two free throws to account for the final margin. Wilsonville's last shot missed as time expired.

The Jaguars, who limited Wilsonville to nine first-half points, got 22 points from McCaffrey. Seth Gearhart, a 6-foot-5 sophomore post player, led the Wildcats with 16 points, 11 in the second half.

Fifth-ranked Hillsboro tied Wilsonville for first place with a 76-60 win at 10th-ranked Sherwood. Wilsonville defeated Hillsboro in both of their games this season. Until Tuesday, Sherwood wa

More articles including the girls' basketball team again.

APPENDIX 9
(*ST. JOHNS REVIEW* MAR. 23, 2007)

The community newspaper celebrates the boys' basketball team making it to state, and earning their first state title since 1954. To God be the glory!

Kris Richards

APPENDIX 10
(*ST. JOHNS SENTINEL* APRIL, 2007)

Roughriders Rising Tide
Basketball just part of a wave lifting all boats at Roosevelt

By Cliff Pfenning

Shortly before the Roosevelt boys basketball team played its first state playoff game in 22 years, principal Deborah Peterson heard something amazing coming from outside her office at the school. Singing.

Members of the team, prepping for their home game against Crook County of Prineville, were singing in the school's main lobby.

"I heard some noise and poked my head out to check into it, and there they were, singing," said Peterson, in her second year with the school. "I couldn't believe it, but what a sight. What a moment."

The Roughriders, before a raucous home crowd, went on to beat Crook County and march to the Class 5A state title game at Eugene's McArthur Court. Roosevelt lost in the title game, but earned the school's first trophy since winning the state title 1949.

While the march to the title game surprised virtually everyone at the Class 5A level and much of the North Portland community, the season didn't surprise the Roosevelt players.

"I knew we had the talent, we just needed to come together as a group to get where we got to," said senior guard Isaiah Johnson. "I'm disappointed we didn't win the title, especially because we got to the title game."

"But, we had a great season, especially when you think about how the school, how the community got involved."

■ RHS basketball is just the tip of the iceberg of athletic success: RHS football has reached the state playoffs two years running and the team's recruitment has gone up from 28 players to 66. PHOTO BY JULIE KEEFE (SENTINEL ARCHIVES)

The team's season helped inspire a community just waiting to show it's support for a long-suffering school marked by poverty and low achievement.

Parents and businesses from throughout North Portland, and Peterson said from other areas of Portland, raised more than $8,000 to

help the team pay expenses in Eugene and send students to games as well.

Danny Ard, who owns a Maytag appliance store near the school, said the basketball season showcased the change in both the school and the surrounding community.

See Roughriders / Page 26

Another local paper states how basketball is just one of the many areas where Roosevelt High is succeeding. The community became so united around the basketball team that people donated $8,000 to help the team—and several students—be able to pay for the trip to Eugene for the play-offs.

APPENDIX 11
(THE ARTICLES STACK UP)

Several of the articles from my growing folder of positive news about Roosevelt High.

Kris Richards

APPENDIX 12
(EDITORIAL FROM THE PRINCIPAL, *ST. JOHNS REVIEW*, MAR. 23, 2007)

A letter to the editor is from Deborah Peterson, principal of Roosevelt High. At the state play-offs, the mainly black team from Roosevelt encountered some negative exchange of words and behavior from white students and adults down in Eugene. Deborah gives her perspective, and states how it was a time for the students to grow through this. The team not only placed 2nd at state, but received the Best Sportsmanship Award. Their responses in the midst of blatant prejudice were stellar.

APPENDIX 13
(KEALAKEHE STATS FROM HAWAII DEPT. OF ED. WEBSITE, NOV. 10, 2011—AS REPORTED TO OUR HAWAII PRAYER PARTNERS)

WE HAVE REASON TO CELEBRATE! THERE ARE STATISTICALLY SIGNIFICANT IMPROVEMENTS AT KEALAKEHE HIGH SCHOOL!

I compared all of last year's (2010-2011 state monitored) stats with the year before. We started doing the prayer walking early last spring.

- 38 less SUSPENSIONS than the year before, from 190 students who got referrals in 2009-10 to 154 in 2010-11.
- Also, the worst type of crime on campus, Class A (burglary, robbery, and drug sales), went down 20%.
- Attendance was up this past year

COMPARING FIRST QUARTER LAST YEAR TO FIRST QUARTER THIS YEAR (SINCE WE STARTED PRAYING FOR EVERY STUDENT AND TEACHER THIS FALL)

- ❖ **Total number of behavior problems last year, first quarter: 93**
- ❖ **Total number of behavior problems this year, first quarter: 39. 58% reduction!**
- ❖ Drug paraphernalia: 6 incidences down to 1
- ❖ Illicit drugs: 8 down to 3
- ❖ Disorderly Conduct: 8 down to 2
- ❖ Insubordination: 21 down to 9
- ❖ Disrespect/Non-compliance: 5 down to 0
- ❖ Inappropriate Language: 2 down to 0

AFTERWORD

Much has happened in our nation and the body of Christ since the big changes happened at Roosevelt High School in 2005-2009. Southlake Church still serves at Roosevelt High, and though the high school has improved, it still is not perfect. There are many schools with prayer coverings that look like what we've done, or even just groups of people who care and huddle together after church to pray. Overall, churches have improved at getting out of their four walls and serving at local schools. What started in Portland has spread across the nation. That is great! But the church has also slipped in some ways into mediocrity and a hesitancy to call sin a sin. We must still remember to speak the truth in love. We love, but there are times we must speak the truth.

As I wrap up this book now from my home in Kona, Hawaii where I serve with my family, I am reminded of a scripture the Lord laid on my heart when we were walking and praying for Roosevelt. It is from Ezekiel 9. In my quiet time this morning, the Lord showed me a picture of a person all in white with a writing tablet at his side. I remembered when he highlighted this passage back when we were living through this story. Ezek. 9:2b has a person dressed in white linen with a writing tablet by his side. The context of the passage is about judgment coming to Jerusalem due to idolatry. The one with the writing tablet was to "go throughout the city of Jerusalem and put a mark on the foreheads of those who grieve and lament over all the detestable things that are done in it" (9:4). The guards came, then, and eliminated all who did not have the mark. When I pondered this passage back in 2006, I connected it to spiritual warfare. I was like that writer, walking through the campus and praying against darkness as God showed it to me.

Today, this passage has more meaning. The mark was based on who lamented and who grieved over the state of the people and their hearts. Though I can't pretend to fully understand this passage, my Bible teacher husband reminds me that it was not written to us, but it is for us.

In Ezekiel 9 the whole difference between those who lived and those who died was if they lamented or not about the condition of the peoples' hearts. Back to Nehemiah, do we even notice the state of the people/schools in our community? Are we sad about their condition? Sad enough to do something?

The other scripture God laid on my heart this morning is from Habakkuk 2: "Write the vision. Make it clear. That a runner may run with it." I have attempted to write down the story of Roosevelt High School. I hope it is clear to understand. Others have caught vision of this model, have had eyes to see plus compassion to do something, and are now praying and serving at their local school. Will you be the next runner?

Kris Richards

ACKNOWLEDGMENTS

There is a bigger picture, a relay race in history, that I have stepped into. I recognize that. So thank you to the two moms in SE Portland who prayed for a year for this. Thank you to Cal and Daniel Chinen who first said yes to praying for Castle High School on Oahu, and for Ed Silvoso who pioneered community transformation in Argentina by mobilizing people to prayer walk. Thank you to Loren Cunningham for listening to God and igniting something in us on our first visit to University of Nations in Kona. Thanks to Steve Duin of *The Oregonian*, who penned so many passionate columns on behalf of the underdogs at Roosevelt High School. Thank you to the leadership of New Song Community Church who believed the timing was right to prayer walk and cover Roosevelt in prayer. Thanks to the

115

St. Johns home group who set up the first prayer cards, for the moms who said yes to taking it to their neighborhood schools, and to the dozens of students and parents who have joined us praying—and serving—at schools across several cities and states. Thank you to the Kona Writers Group and The Write Stuff, aunties who pored over pages on my behalf and cared enough to speak up when something needed changing. Thank you to Benedicte Rogers, my graphic artist friend who did wonders with the cover. Thanks to legends Sandi and Scott Tompkins who first said I should write this book, for their wise counsel and editing. Thank you to my partner in life, Randy Richards, who is just as crazy and faith-filled as me. Ultimately I acknowledge our Commander in Chief, Jesus Christ, who nudged me along the whole way, calling us to something bigger and broader. May He do the same for you.

ABOUT THE AUTHOR

Kris Richards is a teacher by day and writer by night. She has had a chance to speak about Roosevelt High and the simple concept of praying over your local school—and serving there as God leads— in several states and nations. Though she serves in YWAM, she is passionate about impacting her local community (so teaches half time at the local public high school). This is a commitment Kris and her husband Randy made when they got married 23 years ago.

To start up a prayer covering at your local school or learn more about this movement, go to: krisrichards.com.

- To email the author, email kris@krisrichards.com
- Instagram: krisrichards65
- Twitter: AuthorAuntieKris@KrisAuntie
- Facebook: Kris Richards (@AuthorKrisRichards)

117

Kris Richards